BUILDING CHORAL EXCELLENCE

Building Choral Excellence

Teaching Sight-Singing in the Choral Rehearsal

STEVEN M. DEMOREST

OXFORD

UNIVERSITY PRESS

2001

OXFORD
UNIVERSITY PRESS

Oxford   New York
Athenst   Auckland   Bangkok   Bogotá   Buenos Aires   Calcutta
Cape Town   Chennai   Dar es Salaam   Delhi   Florence   Hong Kong   Istanbul
Karachi   Kuala Lumpur   Madrid   Melbourne   Mexico City   Mumbai
Nairobi   Paris   São Paulo   Shanghai   Singapore   Taipei   Tokyo   Toronto   Warsaw

and associated companies in
Berlin   Ibadan

Copyright © 2001 by Oxford University Press

Published by Oxford University Press, Inc.
198 Madison Avenue, New York, New York 10016

Oxford is a registered trademark of Oxford University Press

Library of Congress Cataloging-in-Publication Data

Demorest, Steven M.
Building choral excellence : teaching sight-singing
in the choral rehearsal / Steven M. Demorest.
p. cm.
Includes bibliographical references and index.
ISBN 0-19-512462-6
1. Choral singing—Instruction and study.
2. Sight-singing.   I. Title.
MT875 .D46 2000
782.5'1423'071–dc21   00-020608

1 3 5 7 9 8 6 4 2

Printed in the United States of America
on acid-free paper

For Jessica and Claire

Foreword

Weston Noble

Building Choral Excellence should be required reading for every student of choral music and part of every choral conductor's library. It focuses on teaching one of the most important and difficult skills that choral musicians must master—the skill of music reading. While there are numerous books that offer a single approach to teaching sight-singing, this is the only comprehensive reference on the topic. Dr. Demorest has managed to provide a wealth of scholarly and practical information on choral sight-singing instruction in one compact source. I know of no other book containing this scope of information. It is an invaluable reference for both the aspiring teacher and the seasoned veteran.

The three sections of the book offer different types of information. The opening section, "Why Teach sight-singing?" dispels some of the common myths about teaching music reading and offers an overview of the history and research on teaching sight-singing in choral music education. The second section focuses on the practical how-to information of teaching music reading with a comprehensive look at major approaches to teaching sight-singing followed by concrete suggestions for applying those approaches through exercises and rehearsal strategies. The final section offers a concise summary of published materials to help teachers choose a curriculum that best fits their needs.

Perhaps the most impressive aspect of the book is the unbiased approach in presenting all of the different sight-singing methods. As the author writes in the preface, "The book does not espouse a particular method, nor will it provide you with the single 'best' way to teach sight-singing to your choir." Dr. Demorest trusts teachers to make the choices that will work best for them and for their students. Musical literacy is one of the most important and lasting skills we can give our students. *Building Choral Excellence* gives choral directors all the information they need to develop a strong music reading program, and to give students the skills they need for a lifetime of musical enjoyment.

Preface

This book was written to help choral directors who want to teach sight-singing find the methods and materials that best fit their needs, to encourage choral methods students to include sight-singing in their future choral programs, and to provide additional resources for directors who are already teaching sight-singing. The book does not espouse a particular method, nor will it provide you with the single "best" way to teach sight-singing to your choir. It is intended as a comprehensive guide to the teaching methods, research, strategies, materials, and assessments available for choral sight-singing instruction.

The book is divided into three main parts: *Why Teach Sight-Singing?* This part deals with the reasons, both historical and practical, for teaching music reading in the choral ensemble. Chapter 1 provides background on the long history of sight-singing instruction in the United States. Chapter 2 is a review of research that has been done on the benefits and challenges of teaching sight-singing in the choral program and discusses the implications for choral teachers. *How to Teach Sight-Singing.* This part deals with the mechanics of teaching music-reading skills. Chapter 3 is an overview of the most prevalent sight-singing methods and syllable systems in use today. Chapter 4 presents a wide variety of lesson models for teaching groups at different levels, as well as a number of sight-singing games to enhance instruction. Chapter 5 offers strategies for integrating sight-singing opportunities throughout the choral rehearsal rather than solely as separate exercises. Chapter 6 provides assessment strategies for evaluating both individual and group achievement to help teachers identify and record student progress. *What Materials Are Available?* The final part presents and evaluates resources. Chapter 7 is an overview of what to look for in sight-singing materials. Chapter 8 an annotated bibliography of many currently published sight-singing materials that summarizes their difficulty level, sequence, content, method, and distinguishing features. It compares the features of all of those materials.

This book is intended as both a guide and a reference for the choir teacher. Readers are encouraged to explore the chapters in any order as the need arises. The primary goal of the book is to encourage choral directors and future teachers to include sight-singing as an integral part of their choral programs.

I am indebted to the many dedicated teachers I have observed and worked with over the years and from whom I learned many things about teaching sight-singing. A special thanks to Stan McGill, South Garland High School, Garland, TX; Bobbie Douglass, L. D. Bell High School, Hurst, TX; Brad White, Birdville High School, Birdville, TX; and Leann Banton Rozema, Kellogg Middle School, Shoreline, WA. Thanks to my choral methods students who read and provided feedback on parts of this manuscript as it was being prepared. Mary Kennedy's comments and insights on sight-singing materials were very helpful, and Mary Henry at Southern Music in San Antonio was an invaluable resource for identifying and acquiring published sight-singing materials. Chad Kirby did a fantastic job in programming the Web survey and formatting the resulting data. The many teachers who took the time to respond to the survey provided important information on current sight-singing practice. While the survey was done anonymously, some participants agreed to have their contributions acknowledged. They are listed in the appendix.

I could not have completed this project without support from the University of Washington Royalty Research Program, which funded release time for me to work on this manuscript. Thanks to Maribeth Anderson Payne of Oxford for her initial interest in the project and for her patient and encouraging guidance through the writing process. I am grateful for the wisdom and support of my colleagues Patricia Shehan Campbell and Steven Morrison; I couldn't ask for better people with whom to work. Most important, a special thanks to my wife, Karen, for giving her time and unwavering support to this and many other projects.

Contents

PART I

Why Teach Sight-Singing?

There is almost universal agreement on the importance of teaching musical literacy as a means to musical independence. Few conductors would argue against including sight-singing as a part of choral music education, but surveys of choral directors have found that while many favor sight-singing instruction, few devote significant rehearsal time to teaching it. What is the reason for this apparent contradiction between belief and practice? There are several factors and obstacles that may influence a choral director's decision to either include or not include sight-singing instruction in the choral curriculum. Two factors relate to the director's own musical training:

The first factor is the educational axiom that "teachers teach as they have been taught." This plays a major role in sight-singing's absence from the curriculum. If sight-singing was not a part of a teacher's own choral experience or college methods training, they are unlikely to have either the skills or the awareness to teach it to their students. This book is designed to break that cycle by providing current and future teachers with the necessary tools and information to include sight-singing in their choral curriculum. By learning sight-singing pedagogy in college choral methods classes, future teachers may offer their students something that they themselves never had.

The second factor is the possibility that the teacher is not a good sight reader. Hearkening back to the painful memories of collegiate aural skills classes, many directors allow their own insecurity to keep them from teaching this skill to their students. This problem is easily remedied when teachers understand that *the teacher* should not be sight-reading in a choral sight-reading lesson. The director should prepare the lesson ahead of time in order to help the students deal with the challenges of sight-reading. Often conductors who were weaker sight readers make better sight-singing teachers because they are more aware of the difficulties encountered by beginning readers. As a nice side benefit, the teacher often becomes a better reader by teaching it!

Though personal history can be a major obstacle to teaching sight-singing, it is not the reason most often mentioned by choir directors. Teachers often indicate two "mythical" obstacles to including sight-singing in their rehearsals. These obstacles are termed mythical because, while not accurate, they are extremely powerful.

The first obstacle is the belief that sight-singing is boring. Since choir is an elective class, this belief, if true, would be a valid reason not to include sight-singing. What is taught in choir must appeal to students for the choir program to succeed. Observations of good sight-singing teachers in both middle and high school choirs reveal that the sight-singing portion of the lesson is often the *most* engaging for students. There are few things students value more than acquiring a new skill, particularly one that is seen as special. However, sight-singing, like any subject, must be presented in a challenging but accessible way. If the students can meet and overcome the challenges, they will enjoy the experience. Studies have shown that director attitude toward sight-singing is one of the most significant influences on students' sight-reading achievement. If sight-singing is presented as a necessary evil or as an academic exercise (as in many college courses), then students will be bored with it, as they would be with choral literature if it were presented in that manner. When sight-singing is presented as an important and attainable skill that is central to choral musicianship, it becomes an exciting and challenging part of the rehearsal.

The second obstacle is the perception that there is not enough time. This is perhaps the most common reason given for the absence of sight-singing instruction. Directors already feel pressed for time to prepare a variety of literature for the many performances throughout the year. Even five or ten minutes of rehearsal each day becomes precious time as concerts or contests near. Often sight-singing instruction is seen as unrelated to rehearsal because the difficulty of the literature the choirs are performing is often well beyond the level at which the students can sight-read. In the short term, this seems a practical reason for leaving out such instruction. However, in the long term of three or four years that students may spend in a secondary choral program, sight-singing instruction becomes a time *saver* that can actually improve performance. The positive influence of sight-singing instruction on choral performance has been convincingly demonstrated by the outstanding performances of the many Texas high school choirs that regularly appear on regional and national conference programs and the reputation of the Texas All-State Choir. Schools in Texas have been teaching sight-singing regularly for a number of years, in part due to the sight-singing requirement for both All-State Choir and state contest participation. This emphasis on sight-singing does not appear to have hurt the performance levels of their groups.

Choral music educators must ask themselves an important question: "If I am not teaching my students how to read music, what *am* I teaching them?" A parent whose child was in a choir program known statewide for performing excellence once suggested that her son's choir class should not be offered for credit or be a part of the school day. This was rather surprising considering her love of music. When asked why she felt that way, she replied, "He's been in there for two years and he has not learned anything about reading music or music history; he's just learned a bunch of pieces." If we are to argue successfully that music should be a part of the school curriculum, then we must be clear about what is being taught in our classrooms.

The *National Standards for Arts Education* adopted by Congress in 1994 include sight-reading as an achievement standard for choir classes in grades 5–12. The standard for "proficient" students (not advanced) in a 9–12 choral ensemble states that students should be able to "sightread, accurately and expressively, music with a level of difficulty of 3, on a scale of 1–6." Directors must be able to show evidence that such skills are being taught and assess student progress. Beyond the requirements of external standards, there are more fundamental reasons to teach sight-singing. The confidence and independence that come with developing one's personal musicianship are something that last a lifetime.

1

A History of Sight-Singing Instruction in the United States

A small book containing 20 Psalm Tunes, with Directions how to Sing them, contrived in the most easy Method ever yet Invented, for the ease of Learners, whereby even Children, or People of the meanest Capacities, may come to Sing them by Rule.

Commercial announcement for John Tufts's new
Psalm Book, *Boston News Letter*, January 1721

The history of sight-singing instruction in the United States is composed of many different movements and methods, often occurring simultaneously, that waxed and waned depending on the personalities of their advocates or on prevailing educational philosophy. Since the importance of singing "by note" or "by rule" was first suggested to early colonists, a continual debate has raged over whether everyone needs to learn to read music and, if so, what method will best achieve that goal.

The first musical education offered to the general public in the United States occurred very early in the country's history and had as its central goal the teaching of music reading to improve church singing. By the early 1700s the quality of music making in Puritan churches had reached a low point. A contemporary account of the state of church singing in colonial New England by the Reverend Thomas Walter paints a grim picture indeed:

The tunes are now miserably tortured and twisted and quavered in our churches, into a horrid medley of confused and disorderly voices. Our tunes are left to the mercy of every unskilled throat to chop and alter, to twist and change, according to their infinitely diverse and no less odd humours and fancies. I myself have paused twice in one note to take a breath. No two men in the congregation quaver alike or together. It sounds in the ears of a good judge like five hundred tunes roared out at the same time, with perpetual interfearings with one another. (Birge, 1928, p. 5)

Pastors who wanted any singing in their church, much less good singing, had an uphill battle in the Puritan church, which often questioned the "godliness" of singing. Clergy such as John Cotton, Thomas Symmes, and others worked tirelessly to restore a singing tradition to the churches in New England, and one of the elements they considered essential to that restoration was the ability to sing "by note." In order to achieve this goal, singing schools were formed to teach congregations the rudiments of singing and music reading.

THE SINGING SCHOOL

The singing school was not a place but an idea that gradually spread throughout New England and beyond. Itinerant instructors, some with barely more knowledge than their pupils, traveled from town to town offering a series of classes in "the art of singing by note." These classes often took place in the evenings, and participants ranged from young children to grandparents. The classes usually met two nights per week, lasted anywhere from two weeks to three months, and involved a brief tutelage in the rules of music, followed by psalm singing. The course often ended with some sort of performance or "demonstration" of the group's achievements.

What method did these teachers use to develop such a difficult skill in such a short time? The methods were as varied as the teachers were, and as the singing school idea grew in popularity teachers (and some less nobly inspired) saw an economic opportunity. In truly American fashion, singing school teachers created and published their own method books complete with musical rules and song material for sale to their willing pupils:

> The tanner, the butcher, the carpenter, the unsuccessful lawyer, the farmer, etc., who happened to have a tolerably good voice, a good ear to catch the psalm-tunes, and aptitude enough to learn the few rudimentary rules which were current regarding note-reading, became composers and teachers of psalmody, and went from town to town to teach music, and to peddle "new and never-before-printed" psalm tune collections. (Ritter, 1883, p. 91)

Two of the earliest and most respected of these books were produced in 1721 by the Reverend John Tufts and the Reverend Thomas Walter. The epigraph describing Tufts's book in the *Boston News Letter* is typical of advertisements that always claimed to have found the simplest and surest way to teach anyone how to read by note.

Despite the plethora of published materials, the content of these songbooks was remarkably consistent, because most were copied in part (or whole) from materials published in England at the time.[1] The standard singing school book included not only music but also method. Each contained several pages on the rules of music, an explanation of the system presented in the book, and an occasional section on singing technique followed by a collection of the psalms themselves. The sight-singing system most prevalent in England at the time was a four-syllable form of movable "do" solfège called "fasola" or "Lancashire sol-fa." Fasola was, in fact, a reduction of earlier six-syllable solfège systems such as the one developed by Guido d'Arrezzo (ut re mi fa sol la) some seven hundred years earlier.

Example 1.1 shows the major scale as represented in fasola notation. The singer need only learn four syllables, with "mi" always representing the leading tone. One innovation, credited to Tufts, was that the letters of the syllables were not printed in *addition* to standard notation, as was common practice, but on the staff in place of the note head. Rhythm in this system was indicated by a series of dots after the letter as seen in example 1.2. Despite the potential confusion of having only three syllables to represent six pitches of the scale, fasola seemed to serve well as a means of teaching the early colonists the rudiments of music reading.

Yet American ingenuity could not be satisfied with only a single teaching approach. As one historian observed,

> That peculiar American trait of trying to reduce every thing that seems complicated, and takes, as such, considerable time to master, to a great simplicity of system in order to learn it quickly, and save time, has also induced many of the psalm-tune teachers to endeavor to devise simple and short methods for the study of the rudiments of music. One does away with the lines of the staff; one changes the position of the clefs; another invents new forms of musical characters, -patent notes; now the flats, now the sharps, are found to be too embarrassing to the impatient learner, and are done away with; the whole staff, notes and all, are swept away, and replaced by figures. . . . And of course we are told, that, by means of such new and "indispensable methods" the study of music will be found to be merely child's play; but after a little while the new system fails to meet the "much felt want," and is after a little trial again quietly put away. It does not prove a successful speculation; and a sensible return to the "old fashioned" method is generally the result of all such attempts. (Ritter, 1883, p. 160)

EXAMPLE 1.1. THE MAJOR SCALE IN FASOLA.

| Fa | Sol | La | Fa | Sol | La | Mi | Fa |

One of the most unique systems developed to aid in music reading was that of shape notes (also known as "patent notes"). This system, developed by William Little, William Smith, and Andrew Law, was another form of movable "do" that used different-shaped note heads to represent different steps of the scale (fig. 1.1). While Ritter dismissed it as a gimmick, it became extremely popular in the southern and western United States and is the only singing school tradition that carries on to the present day.[2]

The singing school had as its two primary goals the development of choral singing and the teaching of music reading. By all accounts, it achieved both of these goals admirably. As historian Edward B. Birge writes, the singing school "laid the national foundations for musical culture and appreciation, the full strength of which did not become evident until the next period" (1928, p. 11). The next period of which Birge speaks was the introduction of music into the public school curriculum in the early 1800s.

FIGURE 1.1 TWO EXAMPLES OF "OLD 100" PRINTED IN SHAPE NOTE NOTATION FROM ANDREW LAW'S *THE ART OF SINGING IN THREE PARTS* (1803) AND *SELECT HARMONY* (1812).

SIGHT-SINGING IN AMERICAN PUBLIC EDUCATION

Lowell Mason

As American education developed, people concerned with music and the arts began to seek a place for them in the school curriculum. The first formal acceptance of music instruction into any public school occurred in Boston, where Lowell Mason, a famous singing school instructor and successful composer/compiler of songbooks, taught music for free for a year to prove that all children could learn and benefit from music instruction. Mason became an influential figure in music pedagogy. Having learned of the ideas of European teachers such as Pestalozzi and Froebel, he advocated the idea that children should sing by rote (or imitation) first before learning the rules of music reading. His argument was that they should be comfortable as singers and familiar with the sounds of music before connecting those sounds to a symbol. While this may seem extremely logical and is common practice today, remember that the "note" approach to singing, advocated by most teachers up to this point, had students study the rules of notation prior to attempting to sing. Mason also advocated the use of a seven-syllable movable "do" solfège (do re mi fa sol la si) in contrast to the more common four-syllable fasola.

Mason's method of teaching, complete with solfège and song material, was published in 1834 in the influential *Manual of the Boston Academy of Music, for Instruction in the Elements of Vocal Music, on the System of Pestalozzi.*[3] After presenting the fundamentals of the rote song method and instructions on how to use the manual, Mason divides music-reading instruction into rhythm, melody, and dynamics, each with its own course of study. He instructs the teacher to present the divisions concurrently so, for example, the first rhythm course and the first pitch course are mastered at the same time. The manual is full of very specific instructions on how to present each new idea. Mason often used multiple representations to get ideas across, with many opportunities for repetition. For example, when he introduces the scale, students are instructed to sing up and down the scale first on syllables, then on scale step numbers, and finally on the syllable "la" (fig. 1.2). An important difference between Mason's approach and many of those that preceded it was the emphasis on developing a sound-based understanding of music prior to teaching the rules of notation. An understanding of the sounds of music was developed through rote singing:

Before attempting to give children regular instruction in the elements of music, they must be taught to sing easy songs or tunes by rote, or by

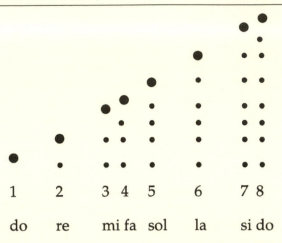

imitation. This may be done at a very early age, in the family, or in in-
fant schools, in which but little more than this should be attempted.
(Mason, 1837, p. 25)

Thus the rote-versus-note controversy was born, and it has lasted until
the present day with some modifications. The debate as it was first developed was never about whether or not students should learn to read
music but about the sequence through which students came to music
reading. Because Mason was so influential and trained so many teachers, the rote-before-note approach became prevalent in the early days of
music instruction in American public schools. However, it was far from
universal in its influence or acceptance. As one writer put it, "A war of
pedagogy was declared almost with the inception of public school
music in America" (John, 1954, p. 103). The battleground for this war
was the music-publishing industry and the primary weapon the graded
method book. Each publisher sought out prominent music educators
to design and promote a series of books that represented different approaches to teaching music reading.

The Music Method Book

While music publishing had already played a large part in the history of
sight-singing instruction, the late 1800s saw an explosion of publications
related to music teaching, with various approaches to music reading at the
core of their differences. Like their predecessors in colonial New England,

these books were influenced heavily by European methods of the time, most notably those of England, Germany, and France. After the American Civil War, music was being offered to students in all grades and there was a need for "graded" music books that offered song material at different levels of difficulty. The first nationally prominent graded series was Luther Whiting Mason's *National Music Course*, published in 1870.[4]

While Luther Whiting Mason was only distantly related to Lowell Mason, he was an avid student of his relative's pedagogical philosophies. Like Lowell, Luther Mason served as a music supervisor in the Boston public schools, during which time he published many of his influential method books. The *National Music Course*, a series of seven graded books, was influenced by German graded method books of the same period and firmly rooted in Lowell Mason's rote-before-note pedagogy, now called the "song method."[5] In his books, Luther Mason used scale step numbers to introduce notation and then printed both numbers and note names under standard notation but instructed the teacher to have students sing on solfège syllables. For rhythm Mason used his own system of time names, which used the measure as the unit of counting, unlike the Chevé system, which used the beat as the central unit.

The *National Music Course* became the most popular music-teaching method in the United States and a prototype for all of the many series that followed. In addition, it achieved international attention and was adopted as a text in both Germany and Japan. Luther Mason's success in teaching a generation to read music was tempered by the fact that his books were often in the hands of the grade-level teachers or poorly trained specialists who understood rote teaching but not the connection of rote method to music reading.

While it would seem that the rote-to-note advocates had won the war at this point, the fight was only beginning. Education at the turn of the century reflected a growing appreciation for the scientific and efficient nature of an industrial society, and the note approach to music reading was now seen as being more "scientific." In 1883 Josiah Holt published the *Normal Music Course*, a scientific approach to the study of music that advocated the note method. Holt's books had an elaborate and carefully sequenced series of exercises for learning to read by note. Holt's approach became popular with educators for several reasons: 1) Holt was also Boston music supervisor and by all accounts a talented teacher; 2) people knew Luther Mason's books well and were looking for something new; and 3) Holt's scientific approach was in keeping with theories of general education being espoused by William James and his followers.

Birge (1928) describes the period from 1885 to 1905 as having an unprecedented focus on "the problem of music reading," but with mixed results. The song methods (as rote approaches were called) did not give enough time to reading notation and in some cases never got to the point of teaching music reading. However, the note methods often produced children who could sing exercises flawlessly but could not apply their skill to real music. In addition to conflicts over approaches to reading preparation, there were numerous arguments regarding the merits of the movable "do," fixed "do," and Tonic Sol-fa systems. The following quote, excerpted from an 1888 music educators' conference, indicates the strength of certain teachers' convictions: "I lay before you the advantage of the God-given system [the Tonic Sol-fa] which I believe is bound to revolutionize the singing" (S. M'Burney in John, 1954, p. 104). As one historian noted,

> American school music teachers in the last half of the nineteenth century revealed an admirable depth of understanding of subject matter, a clear grasp of the functions of solmization and simplified notation in sight-singing instruction, and a realistic awareness of and attention to the special needs of children in the educative process. Their generally lucid and imaginative handling of subject matter presentation, sequence, and solmization, and notation offers much food for thought to present-day music educators. (Blum, 1971, p. 452)

This observation is borne out by the fact that most of the present-day systems for music reading, which will be discussed in chapter 3, were in use in some form at the end of the nineteenth century.

Despite the overwhelming focus on method, some teachers did manage to be successful without advocating any one approach. Birge (1928) mentions two teachers, Sterrie Weaver and Thaddeus Giddings, who had remarkable success at teaching sight-singing but did not use any of the published method books or established methods of instruction. As with the singing school teachers a century earlier, success or failure in teaching sight-singing seemed to rest more with the individual teacher than with any particular methods or materials—an important point for today's teachers to consider.

THE A CAPPELLA MOVEMENT: SIGHT-SINGING IN THE HIGH SCHOOL CHOIR

Vocal music had been a part of high school instruction since the mid-1800s. It was first introduced as sight-singing instruction but gradually developed into choral singing. The nature of the instruction varied from casual auditorium singing for the entire student body to oratorio singing by large choruses. While there are records of high schools in various parts of the country mounting performances of major choral works, most of the instruction was in the form of assembly singing. Historian Edward Birge recalls his own high school music education around 1887:

> I remember that when I was a student at Providence (RI) High School—there was but one then—we boys and girls of the classical and English Departments, so-called, gathered once a week in the auditorium for music. There were no recitations in music, just singing, and the whole hour was very enjoyable, and I think profitable. But this was the entire musical opportunity in that large high school, and of all similar schools, generally speaking, everywhere. (Keene, 1982, p. 317)

By the mid-1920s, vocal music in American high schools was under siege, not from outside detractors attempting to remove it from the curriculum but from a new musical offering: the high school band. While the brass band was popular in the late nineteenth century in the form of town bands and professional touring groups, it had not been widely introduced into the public schools. With the outbreak of the First World War and the attendant need for patriotic and martial music, bands became more prevalent and popular in the public schools. Unlike school orchestras, which often relied on students studying privately, the bands were formed from students who had no prior training. The attraction of the instruments combined with uniforms and parades was irresistible to many young men. In addition, school band competitions, which began in 1920, made band even more appealing and promoted instrumental music to a wider audience. Choral teachers now had to compete with the bands to attract students.

This was the situation in which choral music found itself in the late 1920s. Once the only form of school music, it was now in danger of being eclipsed. Enterprising teachers had to find a way to make choral singing as attractive as band participation. The result was the most noninstrumental ensemble imaginable, the a cappella choir. A cappella choirs had been growing in popularity through the efforts of touring college groups such as the St. Olaf College Choir and through the efforts of conductors like Frank Damrosch and Peter Lutkin. The music of the Renaissance had created a new renaissance in choral singing in the early part of the twentieth century. In 1928 the performance of the Flint High School A Cappella Choir from Flint, Michigan, at the music supervisors' conference was seen as the epitome of what a well-trained high school a cappella choir could achieve musically. Reports from the time express unbounded admiration:

> For real choral singing there is no organization in America that is very much better than the Flint High School A Cappella Choir. Diction? Superb. Shading and nuance? Likewise fine. Bach and the Russian num-

ber they sang were "amazing." No—there is no other word; we said "amazing." (in Keene, 1982, p. 324)

One might expect that this attention to a cappella singing would bring about a significant increase in the amount and quality of sight-singing instruction. After all, without instrumental accompaniments for support singers would *have* to develop music-reading skills in order to learn and perform this music. Flint's director, Jacob A. Evanson, was a firm believer in having students read music, and he was said to have assigned outside practice and graded students on reading performance. However, Evanson's emphasis on music reading was not universally emulated by other choral teachers.

One of the most popular models for high school a cappella choirs was the St. Olaf College Choir under the direction of a former band director, F. Melius Christiansen:

> Many peculiarities of Christiansen's work were adopted wholeheartedly by American choral directors: the spiritual zeal of the church-related college choir; the wearing of vestments; the long, tedious tryout procedure; the flawless memorization of all selections; the hidden starting pitch; the repertoire limited to about twenty selections per year. (Kegerreis, 1970, pp. 322–323)

It was this notion of a small, highly developed program of songs sung from memory that became the model for many American high schools. Consequently, rather than promoting music reading, many schools involved in the a cappella movement ignored it almost completely. Choir directors achieved tremendously disciplined and beautiful performances primarily through rote teaching and sectional drill to learn and memorize parts. In an extreme but not atypical example, the Omaha Central High A Cappella Choir, under the direction of a Christiansen devotee, learned only five new selections one year.[6]

The a cappella tradition, which is evident in some areas of the country to the present day, created generations of choral musicians with beautifully blended voices and high performance standards, who were entirely dependent upon a conductor in order to learn music. Yet while the a cappella movement may not have promoted sight-singing instruction, it was very popular and did help to preserve the place of choral music in American high schools. Though choirs gradually moved away from exclusively a cappella singing, the name a cappella choir is still used to denote the select choirs at many high schools, especially in the midwestern United States.

SIGHT-SINGING INSTRUCTION TODAY

Several events have occurred since the 1930s that have had an impact on choral music education in general and sight-singing instruction in particular: the rise of comprehensive musicianship in the 1960s and 1970s, the rapid development of music technology, the influx of world music in choral repertoire, and the *National Standards for Arts Education*.

Comprehensive Musicianship

Comprehensive musicianship is one of the most lasting ideas that arose from the educational reform movements of the sixties and seventies. It was developed in response to the performance-based focus of secondary music education at the time, both instrumental and vocal, that emphasized teaching literature rather than teaching music through the literature. Comprehensive musicianship seeks a balance among performance, analysis, and creativity in music education. Choral literature is seen as the vehicle through which students learn to make musical decisions, study historical and cultural context, analyze and describe musical concepts, and apply them to their own compositional efforts. In addition, it seeks to broaden students' musical vocabulary beyond European "masterworks" of the eighteenth and nineteenth centuries. The influence of comprehensive musicianship on choral music education is difficult to gauge, in part because it is still being realized. As recently as 1995, a new choral methods book espoused the comprehensive approach (Hylton, 1995).

The focus of comprehensive musicianship on overall musicianship should have a positive impact on the teaching of musical skills in choral music, but several issues have interfered:

1. The "comprehensive" aspect of the training that involves composition and improvisation is difficult to implement because of the lack of such activities in teacher-training programs.
2. The focus on music listening and analysis helps to introduce general musical concepts through literature, but the focus is sometimes more on talking about music than on developing musical skills.
3. The role of performance in comprehensive musicianship is not always clearly associated with the need for music-reading skills.

The conceptual organization of comprehensive musicianship encourages teachers not to just teach pieces but to use literature to explore musical elements through a variety of experiences. In providing this variety of experiences, the focus on skill development is often somewhat lessened. In the best case, students are developing broader musical skills through balanced experiences in performance, analysis, and composition. In the worst case, students spend time talking about the musical concepts embodied in the literature they are performing but do not address the skills needed to perform it.

Music Technology

Technology plays an important role in educational practice. Just as the invention of the player piano and the phonograph changed music instruction by putting increased resources at the teacher's command, so, too, has computer technology begun to change the way music is taught. There is now computer software that can help students learn basic musical skills through drill and practice in a rich musical context. MIDI (Musical Instrument Digital Interface) allows students to record and digitally manipulate their musical ideas without resorting to standard notation.

Drill and practice programs, sometimes called courseware, provide information on the rules of musical notation much like flash cards would but with the added benefit of aural skills exercises. Courseware can offer keyboard sight-reading, dictation and composition exercises, score reading, and aural skills practice such as scale and interval recognition (fig. 1.3). Programs such as Musicware's *Music Lab Melody*, version 3.0d (1997), are designed to evaluate the accuracy of a student's sight-reading of an on-screen melody and give immediate feedback. This program will be discussed in more detail in chapter 6 as a tool for assessment.

FIGURE 1.3. SCREEN FROM *PRACTICA MUSICA*, VERSION 3.53 (© 1987–1999 JEFFREY EVANS)

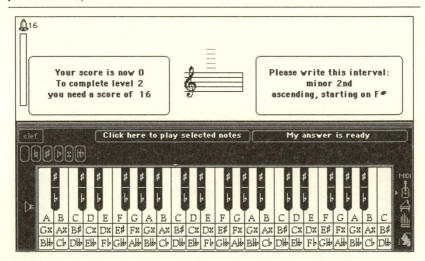

MIDI allows students to manipulate and re-create their musical ideas without musical notation. This innovation, along with other forms of digital recording technology, has changed the perceived need for notational skills. Students can now compose very complex musical sequences track-by-track without ever notating their ideas. In addition, most sequencing programs have the ability to convert the recorded ideas into notation. While this may seem to be a very negative influence on musical skill development, MIDI can actually be a very positive tool for a number of reasons. While musical skills are not absolutely necessary, both the speed and quality of MIDI compositions are often enhanced by musical training in keyboard and other instrumental areas as well as notation. MIDI also can be used to teach students about the interactions among the elements of music and the difference between notated music and its interpretation in performance. MIDI-based programs, like *Band in a Box*, provide excellent introductions to harmony and improvisation in various musical styles. While MIDI can be used to record and drill vocal parts by rote, it also has provided a potential tool for individual skill practice, such as providing a harmonic context for sight-reading (see chapter 6).

World Music

The influx of world music into choral repertoire over the last 10 years has been a welcome and very positive addition to choral music education. It has enhanced students' musicianship by broadening their pitch and rhythm vocabulary and by incorporating elements of movement and instrumental skills into choral performance. Aural skills are improved through careful listening to unfamiliar aspects of musical structure and style. However, many of the singing cultures represented do not rely on standard notation for either the transmission or performance of their music. In fact, notated editions of some cultures' music can conceal more than they reveal about authentic performance practice. Consequently, there is often a greater reliance on rote procedures for learning this music, and the skill of reading traditional notation is less important.

National Standards for Arts Education

It is not yet clear whether the *National Standards for Arts Education* (1994), developed as part of the Goals 2000 legislation, will differ from earlier attempts to identify national goals for music instruction. Historically, "top-down" approaches have had little direct impact on daily instruction.

Music reading is identified as one of nine standards for music education. The national achievement standards for music reading in grades 9–12, shown in figure 1.4, state the criteria for mastery of sight-singing at

FIGURE 1.4. ACHIEVEMENT STANDARDS FOR MUSIC READING, GRADES 9–12 (MUSIC EDUCATORS NATIONAL CONFERENCE [WITH NAEA], 1994).

Achievement Standard, Proficient:
Students
  a. demonstrate the ability to read an instrumental or vocal score of up to four staves by describing how the elements of music are used.
Students who participate in a choral or instrumental ensemble class
  b. sightread, accurately and expressively, music with a level of difficulty of 3, on a scale of 1–6.

Achievement Standard, Advanced:
Students
  c. demonstrate the ability to read a full instrumental or vocal score by describing how the elements of music are used and explaining all transpositions and clefs.
  d. Interpret nonstandard notation symbols used by some twentieth-century composers
Students who participate in a choral or instrumental ensemble class
  e. sightread, accurately and expressively, music with a level of difficulty of 4, on a scale of 1–6.

both the proficient and advanced levels. The difficulty levels for the examples, which are crucial to defining what is meant by a basic, proficient, or advanced reader, have not been identified as yet. Unlike band, no national standard of difficulty exists for choral literature. The best hope for the success of the standards lies in implementing a clear system of assessments so that teachers will be able to evaluate the effectiveness of their instruction and their pupils' progress.

CONCLUSION

It is difficult when discussing recent events to identify particular ideas or moments as *important* or *influential*. It would appear that interest in teaching sight-singing is on the rise based on 1) the number of published materials available for teaching, 2) the increased inclusion of sight-singing in state contests and festivals, and 3) the greater focus on assessment and standards.

The history of sight-singing instruction in the United States offers insight into the current state of music reading in the public school choral program. Since the advent of the singing school there have been numerous methods for teaching music reading, all claiming remarkable success.

No one method has emerged as superior in either process or result. The answer to the music-reading dilemma does not seem to lie with a particular method or approach. Perhaps it lies instead with teachers who believe in the importance of sight-singing and who teach it every day through whatever means they deem most effective.

Music reading has been a central goal of music education from its very beginning, and since that time writers have constantly complained about the lack of music-reading skills among students. In choral music education, this problem seems to stem from our beginnings in the high school as a source of entertainment as well as education. As the a cappella movement demonstrated, success in choral teaching is often defined in relationship to success in performance rather than success in teaching musicianship.

Recent developments in music education, such as a greater focus on technology and world music, have raised questions about the role of sight-singing in the choral curriculum. Technology makes it possible for musicians to depend less on notation to realize their musical ideas; many professional composers are exploring sounds that lie well beyond the vocabulary of conventional notation. Also, as American choral directors become more aware of music from other cultures, it is clear that music reading is not the sine qua non of musicianship that it once was. In fact, notated examples of music from oral-singing cultures such as South Africa clearly point out the inability of musical notation to capture the essence of another culture's music. However, the ability to sing music at sight does contribute to students' overall growth as a musicians— growth that can enhance their approach to music technology and their appreciation for different musical cultures. While recent history has seen many exciting changes in the field, much of the choral literature taught in schools is still firmly rooted in the Western classical music tradition, a tradition that relies on musical literacy. Sight-singing is a necessary and useful skill and should remain an essential element of a choral singer's training.

RECOMMENDED READINGS

Birge, Edward B. (1928). *History of public school music in the United States.* Boston: Oliver Ditson.
Jackson, George Pullen. (1933). *White spirituals in the southern uplands: The story of the fasola folk, their songs, singings, and "buckwheat notes."* Chapel Hill: University of North Carolina Press. Reprint. New York, NY: Dover, 1965.
Keene, J. A. (1982). *A history of music education in the United States.* Hanover, NH: University Press of New England.
Kegerreis, R. I. (1970). History of the high school a cappella choir. *Journal of Research in Music Education, 18,* 319–329.
Ritter, F. L. (1883). *Music in America.* New York: Charles Scribner's Sons.

2

What Research Offers Teachers

There is need for objective research in regard to the methods used in
teaching music reading. When 69 percent of the cities report that
more than half of their classes are unable to read new songs at grade
level, it is a serious indictment of the music reading methods.

K. D. Ernst

Before you skip the rest of this chapter because it has the "R" word in
the title, please look over the following questions:

1. What are the most commonly used methods and materials for
   teaching sight-singing? Is one method more effective than another?
2. What is the most important factor in sight-singing success? Is it
   related to the type of instruction students are receiving or to other
   aspects of their musical background such as outside training? Does
   group sight-singing success translate into individual skills?
3. How much time do choir directors spend on sight-singing instruction in rehearsal? What place do they feel it has in the curriculum?

If any of these questions interest you, then read on, because all have been
explored by researchers. The results of this research will give you information on current sight-singing practices and could help you to make
decisions about how you want to teach sight-singing to your ensemble.

As the epigraph from K. D. Ernst's 1957 survey report suggests, teaching sight-singing effectively is not a new problem for music educators,
and research has long been seen as a means toward a solution. The development of music-reading skills has been an important topic for researchers, though much of the research has taken place on the elementary level where instruction begins. In addition, there has been a great

deal of research on the development of instrumental sight-reading skill. This chapter will focus primarily on studies that pertain to sight-singing as a part of the secondary choral experience. Some of the findings from previous research will be compared with information from an informal Web survey conducted especially for this book.

METHODS AND MATERIALS FOR TEACHING SIGHT-SINGING

A number of surveys have sought to identify the most prominent methods and materials being used by choral teachers. What they found was that no one method or sight-singing book was completely dominant. Several surveys found that the greatest percentage of their respondents used movable "do" to teach pitch reading and that most teachers preferred octavos and self-created materials to commercial sight-singing books. Little attention has been given to rhythm-reading systems in most studies.

Methods

In the strictest sense, a sight-singing *method* should include specific teaching approaches, a careful sequencing of materials, and even a teaching philosophy. Most often, however, teachers use the term *method* to mean the syllable system they use to represent pitch notation. For example, teachers often say that they use the movable "do" or number *method*.

There are a great variety of pitch-reading systems used by teachers, but the most commonly mentioned are: 1) movable "do," 2) numbers, 3) fixed "do," and 4) intervals. G. J. B. Johnson's survey (1987) had directors rank the systems used in their programs. The choices were fixed "do," movable "do," numbers, and intervals. Intervals were used most frequently to teach pitch relationships, followed by numbers and movable "do." There was little difference in the rankings of those three systems, but they all were used much more frequently than fixed "do."

J. A. May's 1993 study of Texas choral programs found that movable "do" was used by an overwhelming 82% of the teachers who responded. The remaining systems were used by between 1 and 9% of the sample. In addition, he found that 68% of the directors who used movable "do" also used a relative minor (minor "la") approach.

Materials

Surveys do not always deal directly with the question of what materials are used to teach music reading. There seems to be a general sense on the part of researchers and teachers that any material will suffice; it is the method that matters. Of the studies that report materials, the results reveal a somewhat consistent pattern. Few directors use materials published especially for sight-singing instruction, preferring to use octavos or to create their own exercises (Hales 1961; Johnson, 1987; May, 1993). May's study reported that approximately 50% of Texas directors who responded used the Oxford *Folk Song Sight Singing Series* books 1 and 2 (of 10). As in B. Hale's study, the most frequently used materials were those not specifically designed for sight-singing instruction unless created by the teacher. No research was found that examined whether or not the use of sequential materials might benefit students' performance over the approach of using selected octavos.

Comparing Effectiveness

A number of experimental studies have yielded mixed results when comparing the effectiveness of various methods of music-reading instruction at the elementary level (Colley, 1987; Hammer, 1961; Hutton, 1953; Klemish, 1970; Kyme, 1960; Martin, 1991; O'Brien, 1969). One possible reason for this lack of consistency in the findings may be the difficulty of separating the effectiveness of a particular approach from the effectiveness of the teacher using it. Comparable experiments have not been done on the effectiveness of specific methods in the secondary choral ensemble. However, there have been some comparisons of the sight-singing achievement of choirs using different approaches. These comparisons are less conclusive than an experiment because the groups being compared probably differed in ways other than the sight-singing system they used. Results of these comparisons are also mixed but suggest that there is no one superior sight-singing system.

A recent study by K. V. Lucas (1994) examined the effect of harmonic context on individual sight-singing at the middle school level. This was one of the few studies that dealt with middle school choral students' sight-singing. The sample was 79 middle school students from three beginning choirs at a single school. They were assigned, by group, to one of three training contexts: melody-only, piano-harmony, and vocal-harmony. Lucas found that harmonic context was less effective both as an approach to training and as a testing condition. This result differed from previous research on harmonic context that used college students (Boyle & Lucas, 1990). Lucas concluded that harmonic context, though important, tended to hinder rather than enhance sight-singing performance. Another possible interpretation of Lucas's result is that there may be little transfer in training students to sing in four-part context versus singing alone; thus achievement in one may not be an indicator of achievement in another.

R. D. Daniels (1986) examined the relationship between the group sight-singing performance of 20 high school choirs and a number of background variables, including sight-singing method. She found no difference in sight-singing performance attributable to methods or materials, although teacher attitude toward sight-singing was a significant positive influence. Daniels concluded that "high school music reading instruction is ineffectual and that considerable improvement needs to be made in the high school chorus curriculum" (p. 288). M. Henry and Demorest (1994) compared the individual sight-singing performance of students in two Texas choirs that had consistently been rated as "outstanding" in group sight-singing at contest. One choir used the movable "do" syllable system and the other the fixed "do" system. There was no difference in individual performance between the two choirs, with students in both choirs averaging only 9.87 out of 15 possible points.

Demorest and May (1995) tested the sight-singing skills of students in eight Texas choirs. Individuals from the four choirs taught using fixed "do" scored an average of 8.79 on the 15-point major melody, similar to Henry and Demorest's result. The movable "do" choir members had a significantly higher average score of 12.89. This difference in performance between students who used the two systems obviously contradicted previous results. We were careful to note that there were other differences between the choirs, such as consistency of training (K–12) and amount of individual assessment used in each program. For example, directors of the movable "do" choirs that participated in the study used a systematic program of individual testing throughout the semester and included sight-singing as an important part of students' grades. We suggested the possibility that individual testing rather than the sight-singing system was the cause of the difference in scores.

If the instructional approaches and materials used by teachers are equally effective in improving student performance, then what factors might account for differences in achievement? Researchers have studied the relationship between sight-singing ability and a number of other skills and experiences. The goal was to determine what aspects of a student's musical experience might influence or even predict superior sight-singing performance.

FACTORS IN SIGHT-SINGING SUCCESS

One of the earliest studies of sight-singing achievement was done in 1940 by E. Thayer Gaston. Gaston found that out of 250 students in 10 high schools, *none* could sight-read a fifth-grade-level melody. A 1957 survey of music supervisors (Ernst) reports a similar lack of ability, with 69% of the cities reporting that half or more of the intermediate students could not read new songs at grade level. Out of five studies done between 1959 and 1980, none found a relationship between choir participation and musical achievement related to sight-singing (Carey, 1959; May & Elliott, 1980; Rodeheaver, 1972; Tucker, 1969; Zimmerman, 1962).

The same studies that have found little relationship between students' sight-singing success and their choral training have also examined the possibility that other types of musical training are related to sight-singing ability and musical achievement. The results reveal that both piano training and, to a lesser extent, instrumental experience are strongly related to both sight-singing and musical achievement, especially when combined with some kind of choral experience. They also have found that success in group sight-singing does not guarantee individual success.

Perhaps the most comprehensive study was R. Colwell's 1963 investigation of the musical achievement of 4,000 students who participated in vocal and instrumental music in grades 5–12 over the course of a school year. While instrumental students consistently showed higher achievement than vocal students, students who received piano training, whether in instrumental or vocal music, showed higher achievement than those who did not:

> Throughout the entire study indications were present that piano training is the most significant factor in high achievement. For example, when sixth grade vocal-piano students and instrumental students were compared, four items were not significantly different: grade average, intelligence quotient, music aptitude and attitude. In the area of achievement measured by the Knuth tests and by the grades given in classroom music, however, the piano students were significantly higher. (Colwell, 1963, p. 128)

Studies done prior to Colwell's by W. E. Knuth (1933), L. A. Hansen (1961), C. R. Zimmerman (1962), R. R. Bargar (1964), and J. R. Luce (1965) also found significant relationships between piano or instrumental training and musical achievement. D. W. Tucker summarized the results of research that culminated with Colwell's study as a hierarchy of experiences that best develop sight-singing skills (Tucker, 1969, p. 96):

1. A wide variety of instrumental and vocal experience with approximately six years of piano experience.
2. Instrumental experience with approximately six years of piano experience.
3. Vocal experience with approximately six years of piano experience.
4. Instrumental experience only.
5. Vocal experience only.

6. General music experience only.
7. No musical experience.

Piano study also has been linked to sight-singing achievement by W. Carey (1959), R. E. Rodeheaver (1972), and W. V. May and C. A. Elliott (1980), and more recent research supports this finding. Daniels's 1986 study found three variables related to students' musical background that best predicted group sight-singing performance: 1) percentage of students who have a piano in their home; 2) percentage of students who participate in All-State Chorus; and 3) percentage of students who had experience playing a musical instrument. A number of studies that measured individual sight-singing achievement (Henry & Demorest, 1994; Demorest & May, 1995; Nolker, 1996) have found that both piano study and instrumental experience are significantly related to individual sight-singing performance.

Group and Individual Success

Even when music reading is taught in a choral setting, its effect on individual sight-singing performance is questionable. Peggy Bennett (1984) suggests that as few as one student in an ensemble may actually be reading during group exercises, with the rest following in close imitation. Several studies have indicated that group success alone was not a valid indicator of individual sight-singing achievement. They recommended that teachers incorporate more individual testing into their sight-reading programs in order to get a clearer picture of individual skill development. Perhaps the most revealing test of the relationship between group and individual success was a study by B. Nolker (1996) that examined the individual sight-singing skills of 101 students sampled from six Missouri choirs. Three of the choirs had received Superior (I) ratings in group sight-singing at contest, and three had received an Excellent (II) rating. There was no difference in the average individual sight-singing performance between the two groups.

Individual Assessment

In a 1998 study, I examined the possible effect of individual assessment as a tool to develop individual sight-singing skill in a semester-long experimental study of six Washington high school choral programs (Demorest, 1998a). All 12 choirs in the study were receiving group sight-singing instruction. Six of these choirs were randomly assigned to an experimental group that received three individual sight-singing tests during the semester. I found that regular individual testing and feedback in connection with group instruction resulted in significant improvement in individual sight-singing performance even under different testing conditions. This finding is particularly interesting in light of the reported lack of evaluation procedures in many choral programs. Daniels (1988) noted that directors rarely evaluate the individual achievement of their students in order to determine the effectiveness of their own approaches. This observation is supported by research of B. Hales (1961) and Johnson (1987), who found that teachers did little formal individual evaluation of sight-singing. My results suggested that evaluation would not only give us a clearer picture of students' individual progress but also could serve as a tool to facilitate that progress (Demorest, 1998a).

TIME SPENT TEACHING SIGHT-SINGING

The importance of music literacy as a goal of music education has been well established in articles and curriculum documents. But how much time is actually spent teaching the skills of music literacy? Researchers have tried to determine what place sight-singing has in a typical high school choral program. The answer has been that while many directors agree on the importance of sight-singing instruction, not all spend significant rehearsal time developing the skill. This may be a direct reflection of the perception (however inaccurate) that teaching sight-singing might hamper the quality of choral performances by taking away instructional time that could be spent preparing literature. As Daniels (1988) notes, "The development of competency in sight reading is a subject that is frequently neglected in the field of choral music" (p. 22). Surveys and other research on instructional objectives and the use of rehearsal time in secondary choral programs have generally supported Daniels's statement.

A 1961 survey of high school choir directors in the Rocky Mountain states by Hales asked about the place of music-reading instruction in their programs. A majority of the directors supported the importance of teaching music reading; 70% believed it should be taught in all choral groups, 80% believed it should be a part of students' grades, and 67% approved of including it in festivals and competitions. However, only 37% listed the teaching of music reading as a major objective of their own choral program. Twenty percent allowed no time for music reading in any of their choruses, while up to 59% allowed no time in their most advanced groups. The primary reasons given were lack of rehearsal time and performance demands.

More recent surveys of choir directors in the North Central Region (Johnson, 1987), the Southeast Region (Daniels, 1988), and Texas (May, 1993) have found various levels of rehearsal time committed to sight-singing instruction. Time spent on sight-singing per rehearsal ranged from less than 5 minutes up to an average of over 11 minutes for the Texas study. This higher average may be a result of the sight-singing requirement that is part of all choir contests in Texas.[1] All surveys reported that directors spend less time on sight-singing in advanced groups than in beginning groups. This was attributed not to a lack of need in the advanced group but to a lack of time given the more demanding performance schedule.

Only two studies were found that observed choir teachers' rehearsals and reported the time spent on sight-singing. C. E. Szabo (1992) spent one week each with 10 high school choir directors from the midwestern and eastern parts of the country to describe all aspects of their professional lives. During his time with each teacher, *none* of them taught music reading as a part of their rehearsals. J. K. Brendell (1996) was interested in how teachers used rehearsal time from the initial bell to the beginning of rehearsing literature. She observed and recorded time usage for the high school choir rehearsals of 33 Florida teachers and found that the largest percentage of *pre*–literature rehearsal time was devoted to sight-singing instruction! She attributed this high percentage for sight-singing in part to the fact that all of the teachers were observed preparing for participation in the same spring choral festival, which required sight-reading, and noted that the procedures being practiced resembled the festival guidelines for group sight-singing.

These studies suggest that while teachers understand the importance of sight-singing, they are not always willing to devote a great deal of rehearsal time to it. The most common reason given for a lack of time spent on sight-singing is "overemphasis on performance, particularly in the select choir" (Dwiggins, 1984, p. 9). The greater amount of time spent by directors in May's (1993) and Brendell's (1996) studies suggests that having sight-singing as part of choir contests may be an important motivator for directors to include sight-singing instruction in rehearsal. Perhaps the requirements for music literacy in the *National Standards* will encourage more teachers to devote time to music-reading instruction. For now, teachers who want sight-singing taught in their part of the country might push for the inclusion of sight-singing as a required component of district and state choir contests.

A SURVEY OF CURRENT PRACTICE

An informal survey, conducted via the World Wide Web, asked choral directors questions about the time spent teaching music reading, the methods used to teach it, and the materials they prefer.[2] The purpose was to provide a current reference point for comparing some of the conclusions drawn from previous research. However, the survey results should be interpreted with caution. While the 178 directors who answered the survey were spread throughout the United States and Canada, they may not be typical given their access to the World Wide Web and their interest in sight-singing. For example, only 20 out of 178 respondents to the survey (11%), answered that they did not teach sight-singing, so it is likely that those who *did* teach sight-singing were more motivated to respond.

Methods and Materials

In prior surveys, no methods or materials were found to be dominant. The Web survey asked directors to choose the pitch- and rhythm-reading systems that best represented their approach using a pull-down menu as seen in figure 2.1. Fifty-eight percent of directors used movable "do," with the majority favoring minor "la," followed by 21% of directors using numbers. The remaining 21% were split between fixed "do" (4%), neutral syllables (9%), and other. Forty-five percent of directors used some variation of a counting system to read rhythm, while 20% use syllables (e.g., ta-ti). The rest were split between neutral syllables (8%), Gordon's syllables (2%), and other. Though the level of agreement for rhythm reading was similar to that for pitch, there were many more subtle variations on the basic systems reported for rhythm. Based on this limited sample, it would appear that the majority of choir teachers use movable "do" for pitch reading and counting for rhythm reading.

Directors were also asked to identify how frequently they used any of 27 types of sight-singing materials, including chorales and octavos. More detailed attention will be given to their responses in chapter 7, but it is safe to say that no one commercial publication was dominant, with the four most popular being used in any capacity by fewer than 30% of the sample. This compares to over 50% who used either self-created materials or octavos.

A consideration when choosing a method mentioned in the Demorest and May study (1995) was the importance of knowing how the students had been taught prior to entering the secondary choir. Ideally, the secondary experience should be a continuation of music-reading instruction, not the beginning of it. If secondary teachers are using an approach that differs considerably from the students' early experiences, much of what they have learned may be lost.

Individual Assessment

It seems clear from studies of individual sight-singing performance that group success does not guarantee individual skill development. Teach-

FIGURE 2.1. WEB SURVEY OF PITCH- AND RHYTHM-READING SYSTEMS.

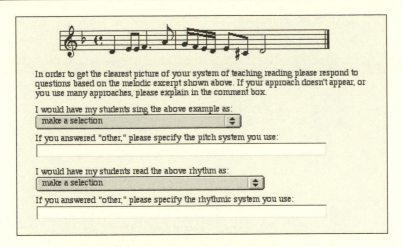

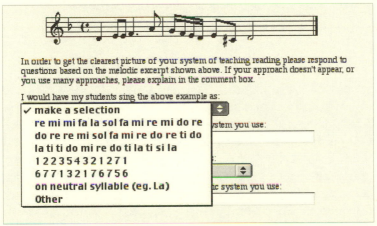

ers must make an effort to assess students' individual progress as well as monitor group performance. As one study indicated (Demorest 1998a), individual testing not only provides evidence of students' progress; it also serves as an effective tool for developing individual sight-singing skills.

In the Web survey, directors were asked about both the type and frequency of assessment used in their ensembles and whether or not sight-singing was a part of students' grades (fig. 2.2). The majority of directors (75%) reported doing some kind of sight-singing test during the year, though only 39% reported doing formal as opposed to informal evaluation. Thirty-three percent of directors reported testing students at least three times per year. Evaluation procedures were distributed between sight-singing alone in rehearsal (12%), alone on tape (11%), alone for

FIGURE 2.2. WEB SURVEY QUESTIONS REGARDING SIGHT-SINGING ASSESSMENT.

---

1. Students in choir are tested individually on sight-singing
   _____ times a year.   zero
                               one
                               two
                               three

If you do individual evaluation please answer the following questions:
2. The evaluation is:
   formal_____ informal_____
3. Students are tested by: sight-singing alone in rehearsal
                              sight-singing alone on tape
                              sight-singing alone for the teacher
                              sight-singing in quartets in rehearsal
                              sight-singing in quartets on tape
                              sight-singing in quartets for the teacher
                              other
4. Sight-singing is 0–100% of the choir students' grade.

---

the teacher (30%), in quartets (17%), and other. While 64% of directors counted sight-singing in students' grades, only 33% counted it for
more than 10%.

Based on these results, it would seem that individual assessment is
becoming a more central part of choral sight-singing instruction, perhaps
due to the influence of the *National Standards*. One wonders whether
including sight-singing in the students' grades has a positive effect on
performance and which of the evaluation procedures mentioned is most
beneficial. These are questions for future research.

Time Spent Teaching Sight-Singing

The data mentioned earlier in the chapter suggest an inverse relationship between the amount of performing an ensemble does and the
amount of sight-singing training the members receive. This would not
be a problem if members of top ensembles had already developed ade-
quate sight-singing skills, but studies of individual achievement in sight-
singing suggest otherwise.

In this survey, directors were asked how many choirs were in their
program and how many received sight-singing instruction. They were
then asked to identify the choir in which sight-singing was taught most
and to complete the answers to the statements shown in figure 2.3 in
reference to that choir.

FIGURE 2.3. WEB SURVEY QUESTIONS REGARDING FREQUENCY OF SIGHT-SINGING INSTRUCTION.

1. I teach sight-singing more:
   all through the year
   in the beginning of the year
   in the middle of the year
   in the end of the year
2. During the time I teach it the most we sight-sing:
   every rehearsal
   almost every rehearsal
   several rehearsals/month
   other
3. I teach sight-singing primarily:
   at the very beginning of rehearsal
   after warm-ups
   in the middle of rehearsal
   at the end of rehearsal
4. I teach sight-singing primarily:
   1. as exercises separate from literature
   2. as a part of rehearsing literature
      both but more 1 than 2
      both but more 2 than 1
5. I spend an average of 1–20 minutes on sight-reading when I include it in rehearsal.

Of the directors who taught sight-singing, well over half reported teaching sight-singing equally to all their groups, a change from earlier surveys. The majority reported teaching sight-singing all year, with 31% teaching it at every rehearsal and 52% at *almost* every rehearsal. Seventy-two percent of directors choose to teach sight-singing after warm-ups, and a majority reported teaching sight-singing primarily as separate from the literature but occasionally as a part of rehearsal. Respondents spent an average of 9.4 minutes per rehearsal on sight-singing instruction.

Previous research (May, 1993; Brendell, 1996) also suggested a possible relationship between time spent on sight-singing and sight-singing requirements for contest. This survey asked directors whether or not sight-singing was an adjudicated part of their large group contest. Eighty-nine of the directors who responded (exactly 50%) had sight-singing as a part of their choral contests. An analysis was done to compare the average rehearsal time spent teaching sight-singing between contest and non–contest directors. Contest directors spent significantly more time on sight-singing ($p = .0001$), with an average of 10 minutes per rehearsal compared with 7.22 minutes for non–contest directors. Contest directors also included sight-singing as a significantly higher percentage of students' grades ($p = .003$). It would seem that the inclusion of sight-singing in contests may be an effective way to motivate directors to spend rehearsal time developing the skill.

CONCLUSION

While this review of research is not exhaustive, it does provide a good starting point for understanding the kinds of questions that have been asked and what has been found thus far. It seems clear that there is not one method or material that guarantees success in teaching music reading. In fact, a positive attitude about sight-singing may be the most effective instructional tool. Based on the studies reviewed, teachers interested in increasing the effectiveness of choral training for developing sight-singing skills need to: 1) commit rehearsal time to teaching sight-singing, perhaps advocating its use in choral contests; 2) attempt to incorporate the benefits of both keyboard and instrumental training into a more comprehensive curriculum; and 3) make provisions for systematic individual evaluation of their students' ability.

The most important decision a teacher makes may be the decision to teach sight-singing on a regular basis. Daniels (1986) identified teachers' attitudes toward sight-singing as an important variable in group sight-singing success. Attitude can contribute in a number of ways. First, demonstrating genuine enthusiasm for an activity will always yield better results with students than taking a workmanlike approach. Enthusiastic teachers are likely to be more creative in presenting sight-singing challenges to their students. Second, teachers who believe in the importance of sight-singing are more likely to devote rehearsal time to its development and tie it to various aspects of their rehearsals.

The background variable most consistently and strongly related to achievement is piano training. One look at the layout of the keyboard suggests that it has enormous potential for teaching musical relationships, and the ability to have both melodic and harmonic experiences in one instrument cannot be discounted. Perhaps choral directors should seek to incorporate some basic keyboard training into their choral programs through the use of electronic keyboards. They are compact and portable and provide a very accessible medium for learning basic concepts of key and scale relationships. Students could work in groups where more-experienced students help the less-experienced students. The addition of computers could provide opportunities for composition as well as skill development. Keyboard instruction may be an important component of a more comprehensive choral music education, and this is certainly an area in which more research is needed.

Instrumental experience was related to better sight-singing performance more often than choral experience in many studies. In most of these studies, students with an instrumental background were also singing in a choir, so one cannot ignore the possibility that the combination of experiences was important, not just the instrumental experience alone. If this is true, then it argues against the either/or choices our students are regularly forced to make between vocal and instrumental participation.

Perhaps the difference is not in the instrumental training itself but in the discipline that comes with expectations and priorities of the instrumental ensemble. Choral teachers might benefit from looking at the structure and activities of instrumental programs as a guide for improving reading instruction in the choral ensemble. For example, instrumental groups often feature private and small group lessons that involve not just playing skills but also instruction in reading musical notation. Students are expected to practice at home, and there are a variety of graded method books for individual study. The incorporation of keyboard skills and instrumental curriculum models requires a broadening of current ideas regarding what choral training should be, but they hold the promise of many rewards for students.

RECOMMENDED READINGS

Colwell, R. (1963). An investigation of musical achievement among vocal students, vocal-instrumental students, and instrumental students. *Journal of Research in Music Education, 11,* 123–130.

Daniels, R. D. (1988). Sight-reading instruction in the choral rehearsal. *Update: Applications of Research in Music Education, 6* (2), 22–24.

Demorest, S. M. (1998). Sight-singing in the secondary choral ensemble: A review of the research. *Bulletin of the Council for Research in Music Education, 137,* 1–15.

Hodges, D. (1992). The acquisition of music reading skills. In R. Colwell (Ed.) *Handbook of research on music teaching and learning* (pp. 466–471). New York: Schirmer.

PART II

How to Teach Sight-Singing

This book is intended as a reference to help choir directors make informed choices about teaching sight-singing in their choir program. The chapters in Part II focus on how sight-singing may be taught. Few topics have provoked more impassioned debate among music teachers than that of the "best" method to teach sight-singing. Educators often feel strongly about the approaches they use and have "evidence" to support their claims. However, the historical and empirical evidence presented thus far does not seem to support any claim of methodological superiority. For that reason, this book does not endorse any one method of teaching music reading but instead seeks to present an overview of choices for the teacher to make. The information in this part is based on two underlying beliefs:

1. There is no single best way to teach sight-singing.
2. All sight-singing methods are a means to an end, not an end in themselves.

There is no single best way to teach sight-singing. While this may seem a strange claim to read in a sight-singing book, it is the view best supported by the evidence. Discovering *the* method for teaching music reading has been a sort of Holy Grail for music educators, and we have expended a great deal of energy on an issue that may not be an issue. Perhaps the preceding statement would best be phrased: "There are *many* right ways to teach sight-singing." This is a crucial point for teachers who seek an approach to teaching music reading. Many books on sight-singing claim to offer the "best" approach and one that has been "proven" to work, and those claims are largely true *for that author.* More important than any method is the teacher who uses it. If teachers find an approach that is logical, sensible, and comfortable to them, then they are more likely to use it often and to teach it clearly. Those last two aspects may be the most important factors in successful sight-singing: teaching it often and teaching it clearly.

All sight-singing methods are a means to an end, not an end in themselves. In an excellent review of sight-singing methods, W. Winnick (1987) outlines the strengths and weaknesses of each syllable system in dealing with certain kinds of music.[1] Many harmonically based methods fall short when confronted with nontonal music, but one has to wonder: If singers are at the stage of reading nontonal music, perhaps they no longer *need* a system to help them read. The goal of any sight-singing system should be obsolescence, to bring the singers to a point where they no longer need the crutch of the syllables to help them hear relationships or patterns. Unfortunately, in the heat of the pedagogy wars, method and end result often get confused. Perhaps the clearest example of this was a student with absolute pitch who was taking her aural skills placement exam at a well-known conservatory. She was asked to sing the examples using solfège. She explained that she never learned solfège because she had absolute pitch and could sing without it. She was placed in remedial ear training to learn the syllables.

The position of this book is that teachers must choose an approach with which they are comfortable and employ it on a consistent basis. If this is done, the students will become better readers. Therefore, it is important for a teacher to know what the choices are in teaching sight-singing and what the relative merits or drawbacks of these approaches might be. Chapter 3 will present an overview of systems and methods used to teach sight-singing in the choral program. Chapter 4 presents a number of sample lessons with a discussion of how and where they might be used. Chapter 5 suggests strategies for incorporating sight-singing into the rehearsal of choral literature.

Once a teacher has determined what skills and concepts to teach the students, the teacher must develop a means of evaluating students' individual progress toward those goals. Chapter 6 presents a number of procedures for both group and individual assessment in the choral rehearsal, followed by a discussion of scoring systems and grading suggestions. With quality materials and clear assessments the choral teacher can be sure that students in their classroom are developing the necessary skills to become independent musicians.

3

Systems and Methods
of Instruction

The best teacher will not be confined to any previously laid out plan,
but will from the different methods make out one of his own; not
indeed one that is stereotyped and unalterable, but one that he may
modify and adapt to the varying wants and circumstances of his
different classes.

Lowell Mason

This chapter presents an overview of systems and methods for teaching music reading along with some background on each. One often
hears the terms *method* and *system* used interchangeably to describe
sight-singing instruction, but in fact those terms can have very different meanings. For the purposes of this chapter, the terms will be defined as follows: *method* refers to a complete set of guidelines for
teaching music reading that specifies sequence, content, and particular techniques; *system* refers to the means by which pitch or rhythm relationships are represented. For example, fixed "do" and movable "do"
are two prevalent melody-reading systems and counting on numbers
and reading syllables (e.g., ta-ti) are two popular rhythm-reading
systems.

A method is often grounded in a particular philosophical view of what
constitutes the complete musician as well as in the personal experiences
of the method's creator. Methods are often very specific regarding the
types of skills that are taught, the order in which they are taught, and
what activities are most helpful in developing music-reading skills. In
the United States, it is rare to see a secondary teacher who is completely
devoted to a single method. More often choral teachers in this country
adopt a particular system and then make decisions about content and
sequence using that system, thus creating their own method.

When choir directors are asked what method they use, they will often respond by identifying their melody-reading system: "I use movable 'do.'" However, *systems* carry with them no information on how to sequence instruction or content; they are merely tools designed to help clarify musical relationships for the learner. One reason the term becomes intermingled with *method* and *approach* is because methods often will become associated with the systems they use. For instance, the movable "do" system is used in the Kodály method of teaching sight-singing, whereas the fixed "do" system is used in the Dalcroze method. While the system is only one of the instructional elements specified by a method, it is often the most visible one. For a teacher who is not using a particular method, the choice of system will often influence other curricular decisions regarding materials and sequence. What follows are discussions of the systems available for pitch and rhythm reading and the three major methods that use them.

SYSTEMS FOR REPRESENTING PITCH

The numerous systems available for representing pitches can be divided into two basic groups, those that use *relative* solmization (syllables) and those that use *fixed* solmization. In the relative system, syllables are used to denote scale steps and the first step is always the tonic of the scale. In the fixed system, syllables are used to denote pitch names, and they represent the same pitches regardless of key. Within those two groupings there are numerous variations, many of which are presented here along with some of the history and criticism associated with each system.

Relative Solmization

All relative solmization systems are based on the same idea, that of establishing the tonic or tonal center. Systems with movable syllables are primarily concerned with establishing tonality (major and minor) and the consistency of pitch relationships within a tonal framework. For example, regardless of the starting tone of a major scale, it is always referred to by the same name (e.g., 1 or "do"). Thus in F major f is "do" and in D-flat major d♭ is "do." In this way, the interval relationships between scale steps (e.g., mi–sol) remain constant regardless of key.

Written accounts of movable solfège can be traced back to Guido d'Arezzo in the eleventh century, who codified a system of six movable syllables that allowed singers to read all of the church modes without too much difficulty. Guido's hexachord contained only one half step, "mi–fa," which became the means of shifting from one hexachord to another as shown in figure 3.1. This was useful for the more modal music of his time, but in the late sixteenth century some teachers reduced Guido's system to only four syllables—fa sol la mi. This was a logical development that can be seen in the hexachord shift outlined by the bracket; ut–re–mi in a new hexachord is fa–sol–la in the old hexachord. Reformers felt they could modulate more easily if only four syllables were used, with mi reserved for the leading tone. This gave a syllable to all seven steps of the major scale instead of the six used by Guido (with six notes sharing three syllables). The four-note system gained fashion with English writers and was discussed in Thomas Morley's "A Plaine and Easie Introduction to Practical Music." This four-syllable solfège, known as fasola, was transferred from England via tune books to colonial New England, where it became the system of choice for most singing school teachers.

Movable "Do" Solfège

Others solved the problem of reading major scales by adding a seventh syllable, "si," to Guido's six to complete the octave. In England in the mid-1800s, a seven-syllable system of movable solfège was further developed by Sarah Glover and refined by John Curwen. Guido's syllable "ut" had already been replaced by the more singable "do" (attributed to the Italian teacher *Doni*). Glover is credited with replacing the leading tone "si" with "ti" so that the entire scale could be notated using only the first letter of each syllable. The new system, most often called "Tonic Sol-fa,"[1] still used the idea of relative pitch, so any note could be "do." In Tonic Sol-fa, the syllables were not used to read standard notation; they *preceded* standard notation with rhythm notated by a series of dots and commas as shown in figure 3.2. This choral "tablature" can be found in some British and North American choral music as late as the middle of the twentieth century.[2] The seven-syllable form of movable "do" developed for Tonic Sol-fa is the most prevalent system used in the United States today.

Critics of movable "do" claim that it relies on too narrow a repertoire of tonality in order to be functional. Outside of major and minor, the system becomes more difficult to use, requiring numerous altered notes

---

FIGURE 3.1. A COMPARISON OF GUIDO'S HEXACHORD SYSTEM WITH MOVABLE "DO" AND FASOLA.

							ut	re	mi	fa
Guido's					ut	re	mi	fa	sol	la
Hexachord System	ut	re	mi	fa	sol	la				
Fasola	fa	sol	la	fa	sol	la	mi	fa	sol	la	fa
Movable "do"	do	re	mi	fa	sol	la	ti	do	re	mi	fa

FIGURE 3.2. "AMAZING GRACE" IN TONIC SOL-FA AND STANDARD NOTATION.

s   d   m d m   r   d   l   s   s   d   m d m   r   s

Key F   s | d :—   :m.d | m :— :r | d :— :l | s :— :s | d :—   :m.d | m :— :r | s :—:—

for both modal and nontonal music. Even a standard modulation to the dominant can pose problems in terms of deciding when to shift to a new "do" and when to use altered syllables.

If a piece of music does not have a strong sense of "do," some of the benefits of movable "do" may be lost. Movable "do" proponents suggest reading nontonal music as if it is in C and using altered syllables—in effect using fixed "do." Fortunately, most of the singing done by choral musicians does rely on some form of tonality, and it could be argued that once a group is singing nontonal repertoire, they should no longer need a syllable system to help them read.

Another criticism of movable "do" is that it does nothing to develop absolute pitch and does not connect well to instrumental reading since, unlike note names, the same syllable name is used for different notes of the staff. However, there is no consistent evidence that fixed "do" or any other syllable system helps to develop absolute pitch. As for connecting to instrumental reading, one would have to wonder how a trumpet player's sense of pitch is affected by seeing a c and playing a concert b♭. In fact, some instrumental teachers use movable "do" solfège to help their students think harmonically about pitch relationships for skills like improvisation and transposition. For example, if a clarinetist learns to think of their part (c–e–g–f–d–b–c) as a series of solfège syllables in C (d–m–s–f–r–t–d), then transposing to another key becomes much easier (e.g., d–f♯–a–g–e–c♯–d = d–m–s–f–r–t–d—in D).

Numbers

Another relative solmization system uses numbers (1–7) instead of syllables to identify scale steps. While it is not clear exactly when this practice began, it is associated primarily with the German approach to teaching sight-singing. One of the earliest methods to use numbers in notation was the Galin-Paris-Chevé method (McNaught, 1893).[3] This method, developed in the early 1800s on the ideas of Rousseau, used numbers to represent written pitches with a dot-dash rhythm notation prior to introducing staff notation. Key was indicated at the beginning of the piece (e.g., d = 1), and octaves were denoted by dots above or below the number. Numbers were used instead of solfège because Galin-Paris-Chevé advocated a relative solmization system and in France the syllables had come to stand for absolute pitch names. Though numbers were used in notation, students sang on solfège syllables while reading the numbers (e.g., 1 = ut).

Since that time, numbers have been used to denote scale steps and as syllables for reading. By using scale step numbers for reading, the connection between scales and chord construction can easily be understood. A tonic triad (I) is built on scale step 1 and uses odd numbers (fig. 3.3). With this system, all triads are easily constructed on either odd or even scale steps. Many teachers feel that this makes the recognition of harmonic patterns within a melody easier to grasp. Some teachers use both movable "do" and numbers in sight-singing to help clarify different relationships in the melodies or parts being read. This may have some advantages in teaching theory, but having to be fluent in two sets of syllables would seem to be more difficult.

The number system has all the strengths and weaknesses attributed to movable "do," with a few important differences. The primary criticism of numbers as compared to movable "do" is singability. While numbers represent the same relationships as solfège syllables, the vowel-consonant combinations are harder to sing; *three* instead of *mi*, *four* and *five* instead of *fa-sol*, and the most difficult, *se-ven*—two syllables for a single note. Solfège syllables provide pure vowels and single syllables for each pitch of the scale. Another difficulty with using numbers to designate pitch relationships is that numbers also can be used to designate counts in rhythm. Thus students are using the same set of syllables but with very different meanings and combinations, which could be confusing.

Hand Signs

Hand signs (fig. 3.4) are not really a separate system but more of a supplemental aid to reading. They were first designed by Curwen and Glover to be used with Tonic Sol-fa and later modified by Zoltán Kodály. Using hand signs to represent solfège syllables offers the teacher several advantages. They can drill students on solfège patterns without turning their

FIGURE 3.3. SCALE STEPS AND CHORDS USING NUMBERS.

(5)	(6)	(7)	(1)	(2)			
(3)	(4)	(5)	(6)	(7)			
1	2	3	4	5	6	7	1
(I)	(ii)	(iii)	(IV)	(V)			

FIGURE 3.4. CURWEN-KODÁLY HAND SIGNS.

back to point at a chart or blackboard. Hand signs provide a physical connection to the sounds of the scale, and by having students sign while they read the teacher can watch as well as listen to evaluate how students are doing.

Some teachers believe that the physical response of moving hands while singing can help students internalize pitch relationships, though research on the benefits of hand signs has yielded mixed results. Hand signs are very useful for teaching or practicing solfège away from the board or from written notation. Teachers skilled with hand signs can have students singing in canon or harmony with one group reading the left hand while the other reads the right. Hand signs also can be used to denote absolute solfège syllables. Some teachers begin each lesson by signing "do" or "la" and without giving any pitch beforehand having their students try to sing a C or A to develop their sense of absolute pitch.

Hand signs are sometimes criticized for adding yet another level of complexity to music reading, and one that is not directly related to singing. Not only must students identify and sing syllables; now they must add a hand sign! As one is listening to a group of intermediate-level singers read with and without hand signs, it often appears as though the signs are slowing them down. However, it is interesting to consider the possible role of hand movement in response to pitch as a means of building musical understanding. It certainly seems to be true for instrumentalists, especially pianists, who can often be seen fingering while they sight-sing or take dictation.

Shape Notes

Shape notes or "patent" notes have been used in music reading since their invention at the end of the eighteenth century. Shape notes, like hand signs, are a supplemental system in which the shapes represent movable "do" syllables. Shape notes were first developed in four-syllable form to be used like fasola. Eventually a seven-syllable form was developed that matched the syllables of Tonic Sol-fa (fig. 3.5). While shape notes never caught on in New England or the other northern states, they are still in use today in the southern and western regions of the United States. Organizations that promote shape note traditions, known as Sacred Harp and Southern Harmony, still publish books of shape note tunes. Both observers and participants in the "sings" (singing conventions) held by these groups report a remarkable facility with music reading. Some music educators have suggested that had Lowell Mason embraced shape notes, the future of music literacy in the schools may have been much better, but results from research on the use of shape notes to teach reading to children have been mixed (Kyme, 1960; O'Brien, 1969).

The primary criticism of shape note reading is simply its lack of transference to reading standard notation. Since it is unlikely that all published music will be changed to shape note form, proponents of shape note reading need to demonstrate that sight-singing skills developed through shape notes can transfer to reading standard notation.

Minor and Modal Tonality

One of the primary problems in any relative syllable system is the handling of minor and other modes and representing chromatic pitches. Figure 3.6 shows two prevalent approaches to handling minor modes in movable "do." These are often referred to as minor "la" and minor "do," respectively. Proponents of minor "la" (Winnick, 1987) argue that it rep-

FIGURE 3.5. FOUR-SYLLABLE AND SEVEN-SYLLABLE SHAPE NOTE NOTATION.

FIGURE 3.6. A COMPARISON OF MINOR "LA" AND MINOR "DO" (UNALTERED AND ALTERED SYLLABLES).

Minor "la"	la	ti	do	re	mi	fa	sol	la
Minor "do" (unaltered)	do	re	mi	fa	sol	la	ti	do
Minor "do" (altered)	do	re	meh	fa	sol	leh	teh	do

FIGURE 3.7. A COMPARISON OF NUMBER SYSTEMS IN F NATURAL MINOR.

Minor 1:	1	2	3	4	5	6	7	1
Minor 6:	6	7	1	2	3	4	5	6

resents the relative relationship of major and minor keys and necessitates no alteration of syllables, at least in natural minor. Proponents of minor "do" (Smith, 1987) argue that the association of "do" with the tonic is the most important aspect of any relative system, regardless of tonality. Smith argues that the modes can be learned by the syllables that are altered: for example, C major (do re mi fa sol la ti do) compared to C minor (do re meh fa sol leh teh do) compared to C Dorian (do re meh fa sol la teh do). Numbers also can be used to represent minor as relative to major 6-6 or as minor tonic 1-1 (fig. 3.7).

Accidentals

Accidentals raise another problem for relative solmization systems. Do singers alter the syllable name in some way to represent the altered pitch, modulate to a new "do," or simply sing the "base" syllable and make the chromatic adjustment themselves? Relative syllable systems represent altered pitches several different ways. Figure 3.8 shows two melodies, one in the key and one with accidentals, and how they are dealt with by

FIGURE 3.8. TREATMENT OF ACCIDENTALS IN MOVABLE "DO" AND NUMBERS.

Movable "do"	do	re	mi	fa	do	mi	fa	sol	la	sol	mi	sol
Numbers	1	2	3	4	1	3	4	5	6	5	3	5

Movable "do"	do	re	mi	fa	do	mi	fi	sol	leh	sol	meh	sol
Numbers	1	2	3	4	1	3	4	5	6	5	3	5

a) Typical Movable "do"	do di re ri mi fa fi sol si la li ti do ti teh la leh sol seh fa mi meh re rah	do
b) Winnick's Movable "do"	do di re ri mi fa fi sol si la teh ti do ti teh la si sol fi fa mi ri re di	do
c) Bentley's Movable "da"	da di ra ri mi fa fi sa si la li ti da ti to la lo sa so fa mi mo ra ro	da

movable "do" versus number systems. This reveals another drawback of the number system. Its syllables do not lend themselves easily to chromatic alteration, though some have tried (see Winnick, 1987).

The most common chromatic alterations used in movable "do" are shown in figure 3.9a, with bright syllables for raised pitches and dark syllables for lowered. While movable "do" syllables can be altered to represent accidentals, the quirky nature of the syllables themselves produces some unusual combinations. For example, the pitches e–f♯–g♯–b in C major would be read "mi–fi–si–ti" where the same sound ("ee") represents both altered and unaltered syllables. Creative scholars and teachers have proposed modifying relative solfège syllables to make chromatic alterations more logical and easier to apply. W. Winnick (1987) proposed reducing the number of altered syllables by treating accidentals enharmonically, as one does on a keyboard instrument. Winnick's syllables are shown in figure 3.9b. This would simplify the reading of chromatics to only five additional syllables.

Another, more radical proposal is to alter seven syllables themselves to make their pronunciation more uniform and alterations more sensible (Bentley, 1959).[4] Figure 3.9c shows the altered major scale in "sa-fa." By changing the whole-step syllables to "ah" one retains the half-step suggestions of "mi" and "ti" that denote the major scale. All raised pitches would then be "i" sounds and all lowered pitches "o" sounds. This system is extremely logical in that it retains the half-step syllables and standardizes the alteration of all others. Though both Winnick's and A. Bentley's proposals represent logical improvements to movable "do," neither seems to have been widely accepted. The most likely reason is that tradition does not always respect logic, and so the seven syllables and their alterations will probably retain their traditional, illogical combination of vowel sounds.

Fixed Solmization

Though Guido's hexachord system was originally intended as a relative system to denote scale relationships in different modes, in some European countries in the seventeenth century the syllables (along with the added "si") were adopted as a system to denote absolute pitches. This absolute usage of the syllables began in France and spread to other countries in continental Europe in the eighteenth century. Now called the fixed "do" or European solfège system, it was originally based on "ut," not "do," as c.

Fixed Do

Traditional fixed "do" was an attempt to simplify solmization so that it was less dependent on scale context, which was becoming more complex with the increased use of chromatic pitches and modulations. The use of fixed "do" was institutionalized as the system of choice for teaching music reading at the Paris Conservatoire around 1795. This system used seven syllables (ut re mi fa sol la si) for the seven notes of the C major scale. All chromatic pitches were sung by their root syllable name, so the sequence g–g♯–g♭–g would be sung "(sol–sol–sol–sol)" with the student altering the pitch accordingly. The term *fixed "do"* when applied to the French system is something of a misnomer, since it has only been in this century that "ut" was replaced by "do" in the French system. Modified fixed "do" is the form most commonly used in the United States. Modified or revised fixed "do" uses different syllables like those used in movable "do" to represent chromatic pitches, but each syllable refers to a specific chromatic pitch (fig. 3.10).

One of the benefits of modified fixed "do" is that the issue of what syllables to use for minor modes and accidentals, which is so troubling to movable "do," is somewhat moot. Instead of G minor, the key is "sol" minor, as determined by the lowered "ti" and "mi" (now the "teh" and "meh") and the raised "fa." The benefit of fixed "do" is that the syllables are not key-specific and therefore remain the same regardless of tonality. It is thought that this approach can take students into the reading of music well beyond traditional tonality, where the scale step relationships of movable "do" become nonfunctional. Proponents also claim that fixed "do" helps to develop absolute pitch, though there is little concrete evidence to support that claim. It is important to note that in the French system the solfège syllables are not used to represent the letter names (c–d–e), they *are* the pitch names and are used in both instrumental and vocal training; thus there is one less level of "translation" in using solfège.

FIGURE 3.10. THE CHROMATIC SCALE IN MODIFIED FIXED "DO".

do di re ri mi fa fi sol si la li ti do ti teh lah leh sol seh fa mi meh re rah do

Critics claim that because fixed "do" does not teach scale relationships, it ignores the role of context in accurate singing. Context in this sense means that interval distances change slightly depending on their scale position. For example, the interval "c–e" would be sung with one intonation as the beginning of a tonic triad in C major (c–e–g) and another if it were the leading tone to F major (c–e–f). In movable "do," that major third has two different syllable representations that reflect the scale function: "do–mi" for the triad and "sol–ti" for the leading tone. In fixed "do," the interval is sung "do–mi" regardless of the scale function. If traditional fixed "do" is used, then the confusion becomes even greater as the interval "do–mi" represents both "c–e" in C major and "c–e♭" in C minor, providing no consistent tonal framework. If modified fixed "do" is used, then the challenge is to sing the appropriate altered syllables for every scale but C major.

Letter names

Identifying pitches by their letter names has been common practice in instrumental instruction for many years, but some teachers have used letter names for sight-singing as well. Following the French fixed "do" model, teachers in Germany developed a system for singing both natural and altered pitches that used letter names (fig. 3.11). Used in this way, letter names are essentially the same as modified fixed "do." One of the benefits of this approach is that there is no need to "translate" from instrumental to vocal music reading. Thus sight-reading training in one area is directly beneficial to training in other areas.

Criticisms of letter names in fixed solmization are similar to criticisms of numbers in the relative system. Letter names are not very singable, with one ending in a consonant (f) and many sharing the same vowel sound (b–c–d–e–g). Since the source of letter names is written notation, they do not represent aural relationships in any logical way, so they do not correspond well to a sound-before-symbol approach. Thus a teacher who is using letter names must teach written theory simultaneously with music reading, which tends to complicate the issue and confuse the student. The letter name system is not used much in this country unless it is used to identify pitch names for the interval approach.

FIGURE 3.11. THE CHROMATIC SCALE IN LETTER NAMES.

c   cis   d   dis   e   f   fis   g   gis   a   ais   b   c   b   bes   a   as   g   ges   f   e   es   d   des   c

Intervals

The interval approach is not really a "system," since pitch names are not represented in any way. The idea behind the interval approach is that students learn the intervals of major and minor scales and their alterations and use that knowledge to read music. Proponents claim that it is the most efficient system since it does not rely on key relationships or add the intermediate step of renaming notes with syllables. However, the interval approach carries with it some assumptions about the process of reading music that are difficult to accept. The first is that music can be read successfully note-by-note rather than in larger patterns. Since the interval approach avoids naming pitches, there is no aid to associating common patterns with common names (somewhat true in fixed systems as well). It supposes that a reader can, in tempo, identify and sing each interval encountered along with keeping the rhythm steady and accurate. Studies of good keyboard and vocal sight readers (Goolsby, 1994a,b; Sloboda, 1984) suggest that they take in larger chunks of music at a time, and do not read note-by-note. Perhaps with practice interval readers develop the same sensitivity for notation pattern recognition that good instrumental sight readers do.

A second problem is that intervals, like letter names, require that students have a command of the rules of written notation prior to developing reading skills. Since those rules must be learned prior to aural understandings, intervals are a symbol-before-sound approach. Many directors claim to use an interval approach in sight-singing, but often it is used only to identify a difficult spot or correct a reading error rather than as a system for developing the skill of music reading.

SYSTEMS FOR REPRESENTING RHYTHM

Rhythmic notation as we know it today is a relatively recent phenomenon that emerged in the late seventeenth and early eighteenth centuries. Consequently, the need for syllables to represent rhythm has been given less attention than pitch systems. The most common approach is to simply "count out" the rhythm patterns. This approach, like using letter names for pitch syllables, presupposes an understanding of rhythm and meter notation before it can be used. A number of syllable systems other than counting also have been developed to aid in rhythm reading, though their development is somewhat more vague than their pitch counterparts. Yet another approach has been the use of words as mnemonic aids for common rhythm patterns.

FIGURE 3.12. READING RHYTHMS USING A MEASURE-BASED COUNTING SYSTEM.

Counting

The use of numbers to represent beats in a measure is probably the most common system of rhythm reading. In the standard measure-based approach, a $\frac{4}{4}$ bar of quarter notes would be counted 1–2–3–4. Eighth notes in the same meter would be 1 & 2 & 3 & 4 &. Figure 3.12 shows a rhythm pattern expressed in traditional counts.

The advantages of counting are that students are using a rhythmic language common to instrumental and vocal music and one that is represented in conducting patterns as well. Thus it is easy to discuss expressive aspects in the score such as connecting 3 to 1 or stressing beats 1 and 3 in $\frac{4}{4}$ and then translate them into reading practice.

The disadvantage of counting is that since there is no indication of natural metrical stress or rhythm grouping in the numbers themselves, all such musical considerations must be added based on knowledge of rhythm notation. In that sense, counting is a symbol-before-sound approach. There are some patterns where the same syllables are used for two different rhythms (see fig. 3.12a,b). Also, certain numbers (*three*) are cumbersome to read quickly, though simplifying "three" to "tee" when reading solves that problem.

A variation on the measure-based counting approach is beat-based counting. In this approach, four quarter notes in $\frac{4}{4}$ are now 1–1–1–1 (fig. 3.13). This simplifies counting so that once students know which note value receives the beat, they can often read at the beat level very quickly. However, larger groupings and metrical stress are even harder to indicate because both strong and weak beats are read as 1.

FIGURE 3.13. READING RHYTHMS USING A BEAT-BASED COUNTING SYSTEM.

A. I. McHose and A. N. Tibbs (1945) developed a counting system, commonly known as the Eastman system, that attempted to combine counting with indications of stressed and unstressed beats (fig. 3.14).

Rhythm Syllables

One of the first syllable systems developed for rhythm reading was part of the Galin-Paris-Chevé system of teaching sight-singing developed in France. The system was a modification of the ideas of Rousseau regarding a new system for notating music. It was created by Pierre Galin, a mathematics professor, in the early nineteenth century and later modified by Aimé Paris (a lawyer), his wife, Nanine, and Émile Chevé (a doctor). The complete method was published in 1844, though it had been in use in France since the early 1800s. The rhythm syllables created by Galin-Paris-Chevé were adapted by Curwen for Tonic Sol-fa and eventually simplified for use in the Kodály system. Figure 3.15 illustrates the connection between Kodály's syllables and those of Galin-Paris-Chevé. As you can see, these systems are also beat-based, so that they are easy to learn and use, but do not reveal much in the way of metrical function or stress.

In the Orff-Schulwerk method, the sounds of various rhythm patterns are introduced by chanting familiar words. The idea is to use the natural cadence of speech to develop students' vocabulary of rhythm patterns before they read them in notation. Figure 3.16 illustrates some common words that are used for chanting basic rhythm patterns. While this approach is useful as an introduction to rhythm, it is not effective as a system for reading rhythms from notation.

FIGURE 3.15. RHYTHM SYLLABLES IN THE CHEVÉ AND KODÁLY SYSTEMS.

FIGURE 3.16. WORD CHANTS FOR BASIC RHYTHM PATTERNS.

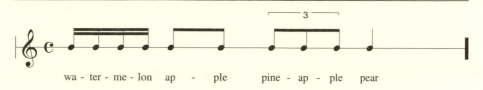

wa - ter - me - lon   ap - ple   pine - ap - ple   pear

Edwin Gordon proposes a syllable system based on McHose and Tibbs that attempts to combine the advantages of beat-based counting with some indications of metrical function. He divides rhythm into meter classifications, and each meter classification has pattern functions such as macrobeats and microbeats that determine which syllables are used. He originally used numbers to represent beats, like McHose and Tibbs, but later switched to the syllable "du" to represent the macrobeats and other syllables to represent subdivisions of the beat. One of the biggest differences between Gordon's system and other beat-based syllable systems is the careful distinction between duple and triple groupings and subgroupings and care with which he attempts to represent those differences consistently in the syllables (fig. 3.17).

The advantage of using rhythm syllables like those of Kodály or Gordon is that they support the idea of pattern recognition. Students see a notation pattern such as and immediately associate it with a syllable pattern, whereas in the counting system could be "1 & a" or "2 & a," and so on. Also, each time value has its own syllable, so the confusion of triplets with eight sixteenth patterns is not possible. The syllables are also very vocal and able to be spoken quickly. Gordon's syllables go even further than Kodály's, clarifying stressed and unstressed beats within patterns, though his insistence on representing different functions with different syllables (e.g., duple versus triple functions) does add a degree of difficulty to learning the system.

Critics of rhythm syllables contend that they simply add another layer of complexity to music reading. Since they do not correspond to metrical notation, they do not translate as easily into discussions of the written score. Many teachers choose to read rhythms on neutral syllables

FIGURE 3.17. RHYTHM SYLLABLES IN THE GORDON SYSTEM.

du   du de   du   de-ta du-ta de-ta   du de   de du   de   du   du da di du

while having students conduct or tap the beat. Émile Jaques-Dalcroze, the most rhythm-centered teacher of all, did not use syllables or counts for rhythm reading. He believed that once rhythm patterns were in the body, they could be recognized and read easily on neutral syllables.

METHODS FOR TEACHING SIGHT-SINGING

The methods most closely associated with teaching music-reading skills are those of Zoltán Kodály, Émile Jaques-Dalcroze, and Edwin Gordon.[5] All three are used primarily at the elementary level, but it is important for secondary choral directors to have some familiarity with them so that they know something of the means by which their students have been trained to that point. Being able to build on previous training can be an important and often overlooked step in teaching sight-singing. All three methods also can be used in secondary choral sight-singing instruction.

Kodály

The Kodály method has been used in this country since the 1960s. It is based on ideas that grew out of Zoltán Kodály's (1882–1967) experiences as a composer, scholar, and teacher. The Kodály method or philosophy[6] of musicianship training has as its primary goal the skill of sight-singing. Kodály believed that music literacy was a central skill and the key to musical independence. His means of teaching that skill are based on the following principles:

1. Sound before symbol. Similar to the historical rote-before-note approach of Lowell Mason, the method starts with music that the children already know well. Children come to school with a vo-cabulary of folk songs they have learned at home. In Hungary folk music is based on a pentatonic scale, so pentatonic relationships are the starting point for music reading. By putting labels to familiar pitches and rhythms in this simplified context the building blocks for future skills are established.
2. Sequential materials. Interval and rhythm relationships are graded for difficulty based on how easily they are learned or sung by children. Folk song material is analyzed for the difficulty of its melodic content.

Kodály employed three systems for representing pitch and rhythm relationships. He used movable "do" solfège and hand signs from Tonic

FIGURE 3.18. SAMPLE KODÁLY SOLFÈGE ACTIVITY.

1. Class begins with students singing the familiar round "Hey, Ho! Nobody Home!" which they have learned previously by rote.

2. Teacher has students chant the rhythm of last two measures while tapping or conducting the beat.
3. Teacher asks students to write out the rhythm in stick notation.
4. Teacher signs and sings: "l–d–m–d–l." Students echo.
5. Teacher signs and sings the natural minor scale. Students echo and identify.
6. Teacher notates the C minor scale on the board, raises the seventh scale degree, and asks what syllable that would be—"si" —and tells students to sing the scale. Students sing the C harmonic minor scale.
7. Teacher asks students to look at the melody on the board and chant the rhythm on syllables. Students chant rhythm.
8. Teacher signs "la" and students sing. Teacher points on scale to "l–d–m–d–l–si–l" while students sing.
9. Teacher sets beat and students sing the melody in solfège using either traditional:

or stick notation:

l t d l t si l   d d r m f mr d t l

10. Have students try in canon (two measure) or create a harmony using

---

Sol-fa (see fig. 3.4) for representing pitch relationships. For rhythm reading he used an adaptation of Galin-Paris-Chevé syllables that used "tas and tis" and developed a stick notation for rhythm that mirrored the stems of traditional notation. Though most of these systems were in existence before Kodály developed his method, they have become so closely associated with it that people sometimes believe that he created them. The goal of the Kodály method is to move from sound to symbol, and all exercises and sequences are geared toward that goal. A sample Kodály exercise for choir is shown in figure 3.18.

FIGURE 3.19. SAMPLE OF DALCROZE SOLFÈGE-RHYTHMIQUE ACTIVITIES.

1. Teacher sings (or plays) an ascending and descending C major scale and has the students sing it back on solfège (fixed "do").
2. Teacher instructs the students to stand when they hear a note that does not belong in the C major scale and sit when they hear a note that does belong.
3. Teacher sings (or plays) an ascending and descending C harmonic minor scale, watching for students' physical response to altered notes. To help pitches "sink in" the teacher could play the scale several times, first in straight quarter notes, then improvising different rhythm patterns such as:

4. Teacher has the students sing the harmonic minor scale on solfège (traditional fixed "do"—no altered syllables).
5. Teacher asks the students to identify the scale.
6. Teacher has students sing an ascending and descending C minor scale several times on the following rhythmic pattern:

Because the pattern is shorter than the scale, each time the pattern repeats it will be at a different point in the scale. Students can tap the beat, pretend-play, or step while singing.

7. Teacher tries this with several different patterns and has the students create new ones.
8. Teacher has students sight-sing the following example in solfège:

9. Teacher has students read again either in major or in $\frac{3}{4}$ time.

Jaques-Dalcroze and Solfège-Rhythmique

Émile Jaques-Dalcroze (1865–1950) was a composer and professor of theory and solfège at the Geneva conservatory from 1892 to 1910. Having noticed that even his most gifted music students often did not perform expressively, especially in their treatment of rhythm, he began to devise a method for combining rhythmic movement with solfège and improvisation to develop more completely his students' musicality. Dalcroze Eurhythmics gradually developed into a method of early musical training where rhythmic movement was seen as the gateway to more complex musical understanding and the key to a sort of inner harmony. Eurhythmics centers on the connection between movement in space and movement in sound.

While Eurhythmics, or rhythmic movement, is the most commonly discussed aspect of Jaques-Dalcroze's method, it was meant to be combined with aural skills training known as Solfège-rhythmique and improvisation. Jaques-Dalcroze, like Kodály, believed in a sound-before-symbol approach, and solfège was used in parallel to Eurhythmics as a means of aural training and eventually music reading. An excellent article on Solfège-rhythmique by Herbert H. Henke (1984) explains:

> It is this emphasis on active and creative participation which sets the approach apart from the more traditional sight-singing and ear-training methodologies. Musical material is constantly being manipulated in ways which demand attention and concentration by the student. The end result is the ability to image mentally both pitch and rhythm, an important component of choral literacy. (p. 11)

Solfège-rhythmique was based originally on the traditional fixed "do" system and centers on students' ability to first respond physically to changes in the music they hear and then eventually produce music from notation either as written or altered in some form. A few examples of Solfège-rhythmique activities for choir are given in figure 3.19. As with Kodály, the sound comes before the symbol and many of the ear-sharpening activities that involve physical responses to musical changes may be done in the complete absence of notation. Pitch relationships are introduced through listening and responding to changes in the sounds of various scales and polychords. Because of the fixed "do" system, all scales are sung "from C to shining C" regardless of tonic. The modes are identified by hearing the changing pattern of whole and half steps. However, there is no reason that many of the activities, which stress careful listening and quick response to changes in the musical material, could not be adapted to a movable "do" solfège.

The Dalcroze method is not as widely used in American education in part because of the need for extensive personal training and the lack of prescriptive materials. Despite a lack of prescriptive detail, it qualifies as a method because of the extensive training regarding how materials should be presented and how different activities should be combined. The "materials" of the Dalcroze method are the teacher's creativity and sensitivity to students' needs. The method does provide many avenues for developing musicality, but the responsibility for the specifics of daily instruction falls largely on the teacher.

The most common usage of Jaques-Dalcroze's method by American choral directors has been the application of Eurhythmics or expressive movement to improve the choir's musicality and expressiveness. However, many aspects of Solfège-rhythmique training, such as stressing careful listening, reading and manipulating written music, and responding through movement, are useful for American choirs, even those that use movable "do" systems.

Gordon's Music Learning Theory

Edwin Gordon's theory of music learning (1988) is based on a very carefully defined sequence of experiences that grew out of his research on children's musical aptitude. Gordon (b. 1927) is a music education professor with a long career of research in this area. His research sought to identify the best sequence of stimuli for developing children's understanding of pitch and rhythm relationships. The resulting music-learning sequence is based on R. M. Gagne's hierarchy of eight types of learning (1965).

Gordon employs a sound-before-symbol approach with prescribed sequential materials. Rather than grounding sound patterns in familiar folk tunes, like Kodály, Gordon developed a hierarchical series of rote pitch and rhythm patterns that he claims will build the necessary understandings prior to encountering musical notation. Gordon also shares Kodály's belief that musicians should be able to understand and experience music internally or "audiate" before they attempt to play it on an instrument or sing it.

Gordon uses movable "do" solfège syllables for pitch reading and his own series of rhythm syllables based on what he terms beat function (see fig. 3.17). In his approach, both instrumental and vocal students spend a part of every class audiating patterns sung to them by the teacher and then singing them back individually. The difficulty of the patterns given to each student is based on their musical aptitude as determined by a standardized test.[7] While students may have been taught this way in elementary school, Gordon has not as yet created materials for secondary choral students.[8] However, his instrumental method involves so much singing that the lessons could easily be adapted for use in the choral program. A sample Gordon exercise based on the *Jump Right In: The Instrumental Series* (Grunow & Gordon, 1989) is given in figure 3.20.

These overviews give a sense of the philosophies behind these instructional methods and their components. Sources for more detailed information on all three of these methods are given at the end of the chapter. Aspects of any of these three methods could be used in a choral setting, especially if students have been taught in the method up to that point.

CONCLUSION

Perhaps choral teachers should agree to disagree regarding the best method of teaching sight-singing, since method seems to be one of the

FIGURE 3.20. SAMPLE GORDON AUDIATION TRAINING

1. Class learns the song "Major Duple" by rote using the following procedure:
   a. Teacher sings the song through one or more times on a neutral syllable.
   b. Students can then echo phrase-by-phrase as needed.
   c. Though no harmonic accompaniment is used when teaching; it can be added after the song is learned. The accompaniment should not include the melody line.
   d. After the song is learned, the words can be added.
   e. Every time the teacher has students sing a rote song, they should set the "keyality, tonality, meter, and tempo" using the following procedure: Teacher sets the tonality on a neutral syllable, outlining the tonic triad followed by REA-DY SING on the starting pitch. This is sung in the correct meter, in this case duple.
2. Teacher sets a different major tonality by playing I V^7 I in the key.
3. Teacher sings prescribed two- and three-note patterns on a neutral syllable (e.g., "bum"). Students echo patterns as a group. Sample patterns on a neutral syllable would be d–m–d | r–t–r | or d–m | r–s. NOTE: The procedures for both group and individual echoing involve the teacher singing the pattern, followed by a pause and breath before the students echo. This is designed to give the students time to audiate the pattern before they sing it.
4. After the students can accurately echo the patterns as a group, the teacher sings a pattern and during the pause points to an individual. The teacher and the individual sing the pattern together in duet (Teaching Mode). During Evaluation Mode, the teacher sings the pattern and points to the student, who sings it alone. The carefully prescribed patterns are designed to sequentially build the students' internal pitch vocabulary. The teacher chooses patterns for individual teaching and evaluation based on each student's individual musical aptitude.
5. The same echoing procedure is then done on these patterns, but now using the solfège syllables.
6. A similar procedure is followed for rhythm, with students echoing duple patterns on a neutral syllable first as a group and then individually, followed by echoing on rhythm syllables, both group and individual.

least constant aspects of sight-singing instruction. What does seem constant is the success of caring and creative teachers who are dedicated to imparting the skill of music reading to their students. It is for this reason that this book was written: to provide caring and creative teachers with the information they need to make an informed choice about the approach they use to teach sight-singing rather than to dictate one method. Several considerations should be taken into account when making a choice of instructional approach. While there may be no single best method or system, there are several principles that seem to be important for successful sight-singing instruction.

The first consideration for teachers is to choose a system or method that makes sense to them. If it does not make sense, then no matter how hard they try, they will not present it with real enthusiasm or clarity. Making sense in this context means that there is a logical connection between the representations of pitch and rhythm used in the system and the teacher's own understanding of music. If the simplicity of having one solfège syllable for each chromatic pitch is appealing, then fixed "do" is a logical choice. Often outside factors influence teachers' choices. For example, movable "do" and numbers are by far the most prevalent systems used in college solfège training, so they may be the most logical starting points for choosing a system.

A second consideration is that for consistency one should choose a system or method the students already know when possible. If a teacher knows the system or method used at earlier levels of the students' training, then building on that approach will be easier than starting from scratch. The majority of elementary method books currently employ some form of movable "do," so teachers need to factor that early experience into their choice. Directors often use systems for representing pitch and rhythm, that are part of a larger method, such as Kodály, but do not adopt other aspects of that method. Training in any movable system will transfer to another movable system more easily than changing from movable to fixed, or vice versa.

Once the choice of system or method is made, there are several other instructional considerations that seem common to all successful sight-singing instruction. Sound-before-symbol or rote-to-note has moved from historical debate to well-established educational practice. Students cannot sing something they have never heard regardless of the number of rules they have learned. All of the major methods mentioned concur on this point, and most teachers approach the teaching of sight-singing from rote patterns to reading new material.

Daniels (1988) has suggested that despite differences in pedagogy, there are really only two approaches to sight-singing instruction: teaching sight-singing apart from the choral literature being rehearsed or through the choral literature being rehearsed. The next two chapters will provide models and suggestions for both of these approaches. Whatever system or method is chosen, the most important consideration is having students sight-sing in every rehearsal and in as many situations as possible. Only this regular commitment will strengthen their skills and convince them of the importance of music literacy to choral musicianship.

RECOMMENDED READINGS

Choksy, L. (1999a). *The Kodály method I: Comprehensive music education* (3d ed.). Upper Saddle River, NJ: Prentice Hall.

Choksy, L. (1999b). *The Kodály method II: Folksong to masterwork.* Upper Saddle River, NJ: Prentice Hall.

Gordon, Edwin E. (1997). *Learning sequences in music: Skill, content, and patterns.* (Chicago: GIA Publications.

Henke, Herbert H. (1984). The application of Émile Jaques-Dalcroze's Solfège-rhythmique to the choral rehearsal. *Choral Journal, 24* (5), 11–14.

McNaught, W. G. (1893). The history and uses of the sol-fa syllables. *Proceedings of the Musical Association, 19,* 35–51.

More, B. E. (1985). Sight singing and ear training at the university level: A case for the use of Kodály's system of relative solmization. *Choral Journal, 25* (8), 9–22.

Szönyi, E. (1973). *Kodály's principles in practice: an approach to music education through the Kodály method.* (J. Weissman, Trans.). New York: Boosey & Hawkes.

Winnick, W. (1987). Hybrid methods in sight-singing. *Choral Journal, 28* (1), 24–30.

4

Sight-Singing Lesson Models

It seems strange that musical instruction has always been begun through the eye of the pupil, instead of through his ear. It is surely evident that we should teach the oral language of music before the written language. For instance, we should not recommend teaching a child to speak by means of reading, or place a book before him to show him how to pronounce words. Yet this is what is done in music teaching: the child is required to perform from written notes; he is made to read before he knows how to sol-fa, that is, before he can *speak*.

Pierre Galin

This chapter presents lesson models for choral singers who possess varying degrees of skill. It is organized sequentially, from prenotational to advanced readers. The sight-singing system presented with each lesson varies (numbers, movable "do," fixed "do"), not because the lesson requires it but to illustrate that any sight-singing system can be used. All of the lessons are designed to be presented as an activity separate from the rehearsal of the literature. Integrating sight-singing into rehearsal will be the topic of chapter 5.

At the beginning of the year, teachers must assess what the students know and can do in sight-singing. If the choir has been auditioned or comes from the same feeder school, then perhaps the teacher has the necessary information on their skill level. If not, then it is important to do some form of diagnostic assessment, such as the procedure discussed in chapter 6. Many teachers, especially in middle school, find that their students know next to nothing about reading music, because of either no elementary music instruction or elementary instruction that focused entirely on rote song learning; they are prenotational. This is the point at which many teachers give up or make the crucial mistake of trying to teach music fundamentals via the college theory model, which often stresses rules and writing before doing. These teachers will tell you that their students *hate* sight-singing, and no doubt they are correct.

There are several important points to keep in mind in preparing to introduce sight-singing to a group of "prenotational" singers. The first is that students do not need to know all the rules or conventions of music notation to begin sight-singing. Students can perform many things before they necessarily understand them thoroughly. For example, they may not know a solfège or number system, but they can accurately sing a major scale. Knowing the sound of and being able to sing a major scale is a powerful sight-singing tool that most of your students should already possess.

The second point to keep in mind is that if you want students to learn to read *music*, use music to teach them, not exercises. Avoid lessons on isolated rhythm or pitch patterns if they do not lead to an exercise or melody being read that day.

The third point to consider is that sight-singing is an act of recognition; the singer sees a notational pattern that reminds them of a sound pattern that they can then reproduce. Thus students cannot sight-sing a pattern that they have not heard. Good sight singers can sing a melody that they have never seen or heard before, but the pitch and rhythm patterns that make up that melody must be familiar in order for the notation to trigger an internal sound model of the melody. As Kodály, Gordon, and others have stressed so often, sight-singing must be a process of sound-before-symbol. That is the central premise behind the prenotational lesson.

THE PRENOTATIONAL LESSON

If students can recognize and sing a major scale, then they can begin to read. To test, have the students sing on "la" while the teacher begins playing the major scale on the piano. While continuing to conduct, the teacher stops playing, and the students must complete the scale on their own. Another test is to play scales on the piano and have the students raise their hands when a note does not "belong" to the major scale. Having established the *sound* of a major scale, the teacher need only put labels on the seven pitches. In the same way, if students can keep a steady beat and distinguish between long and short, then they can begin to read rhythm. During the first few days, the teacher can do prereading activities such as echoing solfège or number patterns and echo clapping or chanting rhythms to prepare the students for the syllable systems they use for sight-singing.

FIGURE 4.1. PRENOTATIONAL LESSON PLAN 1.

Material

Overhead projector with transparency for rhythm patterns and F scale with numbers.

Rhythm Preparation

1. Teacher establishes a steady beat and has students join in tapping. Chant rhythm patterns on counts and have the students echo:

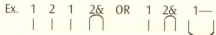

2. Teacher points to the same patterns notated on the overhead. Students chant the rhythm patterns and continue tapping the beat. Teacher has the students chant the patterns from notation in various orders.
3. Teacher shows the students the song notated on the board. Students chant the rhythm of the song on counts.
    (Teacher might ask them to identify patterns from overhead in song before chanting.)

Pitch Preparation

4. Students sing a warm-up exercise on "la" that goes 1–2–3–4–5–6–5–4–3–2–1.
5. Students sing the same pattern on numbers. Students do again as teacher points to the numbered F scale on the overhead.
6. Students sing different number patterns in a steady rhythm as teacher points to them. Include the following patterns from the song:

    1) 1–2–3–4   2) 3–4–3–2   3) 2–3–2–1

7. Teacher shows students the song on the board and has them find scale step 1 from the scale on the overhead.
    Teacher says, "If this is '1,' then what number is this note?" Teacher has students identify other note numbers.
    (Teacher could mark numbers in under the notes at first, but it's better not to.)
    Students sing pitches 1–5 and the 1–3–5–3–1 triad to tune, then sing the pitches of the song out of rhythm on numbers as the teacher points.

Reading

8. Students review the rhythm of the song, chanting on counts.
9. Students sing the piece in rhythm on scale numbers a cappella.
    Option 1: Once with piano doubling, but then do again a cappella.
    Option 2: Once with piano harmony, but then do again a cappella.

→

FIGURE 4.1. continued

Evaluation

10. Students should always try to read straight through without stopping. Once that's done, the teacher can go back and address a problematic pattern or measure and then have students read the whole melody again.

FIGURE 4.2. THE MELODY FROM FIGURE 4.1 IN STICK NOTATION.

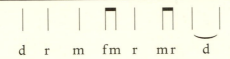

Having students do simple patterns from a solfège chart can be a fun and challenging way to begin their reading experience. As early as possible, however, students should begin reading melodies. The sooner that pitch and rhythm patterns are put into a melodic context, the sooner they transfer to what is happening in rehearsal. Two models of prenotational lessons are given here; both are based on the sound-before-symbol approach. Because the students must learn to associate the patterns they see with sounds that they know, these lessons may not seem like sight-singing lessons to the experienced musician, but they are a necessary first step in the reading process. The goal of the prenotational lesson is to begin to transfer what students hear into what they can reproduce.

The lesson in figure 4.1 moves the students from echo patterns of rhythm and pitch into notated versions of the same patterns. While information such as time and key signatures is present in the notated melody, it is not discussed. Some teachers leave time and key signatures off entirely at first so that they will not be a distraction. If your students have been taught using elements of the Kodály method, then they may not have seen traditional notation as often as Kodály's solfège notation. Figure 4.2 shows the melody from the first prenotational lesson in Kodály's stick notation.

In this type of prenotational approach, the stick notation and solfège syllables serve as an intermediate step between rote learning and traditional notation. The essentials are still there in terms of rhythm and solfège, but without bar lines or other trappings of notation. Students gradually move from this kind of notation to traditional staff notation using familiar songs at first.

Another system used to represent pitches is hand signs. The prenotational lesson in figure 4.3 shows how hand signs and stick notation could be used in a beginning lesson. While the devices are associated with Kodály, this lesson does not necessarily adhere strictly to the Kodály philosophy or sequence.

FIGURE 4.3. PRENOTATIONAL LESSON PLAN 2.

Material
Overhead projector with transparency for solfège chart and stick notation.

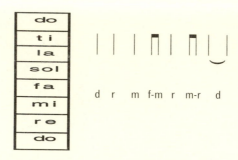

Rhythm Preparation
1. Teacher establishes a steady beat and has students join in tapping.
2. Teacher chants the following rhythm patterns on "tas" and "tis" and has the students echo: ta ta ta ti -ti   and   ta ti -ti ta - ah.
3. Teacher chants the same rhythm patterns while pointing to the stick notation patterns on the overhead.
4. Students echo and continue tapping the beat.

5. Students chant patterns A and B from stick notation in various orders.
6. Teacher shows the students the song notated on the board with solfège and has them chant only the rhythm on "tas" and "tis."
   Teacher could ask students to identify patterns A and B from overhead in song before chanting
   Teacher could also have the building blocks of the patterns, "ta," "ti-ti," and "ta -ah," notated on the board.

Pitch Preparation
5. Teacher has students sing a warm-up exercise on "la" that goes d–r–m–f–s–l–s–f–m–r–d.
6. Teacher then sings the same pattern on solfège syllables using hand signs. Students echo with hand signs.*
7. Teacher has students sing different syllable patterns from the song in a steady rhythm from hand signs. For example:
   1) d–r–m–f   2) m–f–m–r   3) r–m–r–d

Reading
8. Teacher shows students the song on the board.
   Teacher has students sign and sing "do" again, then has them sign and chant the solfège syllables in rhythm.
   Teacher reviews any rhythm problems on "ta" and "ti."

→

FIGURE 4.3. continued

9. Students sing and sign d–s and the tonic triad to tune, then sing the song on solfège in rhythm with hand signs. Teacher signs in rhythm with their singing, but does not sing.
10. Teacher reviews any problem areas. Students sing and sign again while the teacher conducts or keeps the beat.

Evaluation
11. As before, students should always try to read straight through without stopping. Once that's done, the teacher can go back and address a problematic pattern or measure and then have students read the whole melody again.
    * Hand signs can be taught to the students at the very beginning of the year. They will require a lot of repetition in order to become fluent. Some teachers spend quite a bit of time having students "read" only from hand signs before introducing other forms of pitch notation.

Though they use different systems and materials, both prenotational lessons share the crucial sequence of sound-before-symbol. Students will spend a fair amount of time at this level of reading, and they do not progress out of it all at once. As certain basic patterns become familiar, the teacher can begin to skip steps and move through the lesson more quickly—for example, having students scan the melody first for difficult rhythm patterns and, if none are found, read the rhythm directly from the melody without echoing. The same can be done with pitches; after scanning for difficult spots students could read the pitches in rhythm the first time. However, as new and more difficult patterns are introduced it will be important to move back into a more prenotational sequence until the sounds become familiar.

MUSIC FUNDAMENTALS

As students begin to develop a vocabulary of pitch and rhythm patterns that they can read reliably, the teacher can begin to introduce them to more of the information contained in the score, such as note names, clefs, meter signatures, and key signatures, so that they can find the tonic independently, set the beat and the key, and begin reading. This information, when taught through sight-singing practice, will eventually allow the students to figure out the sounds of new patterns based on previous information.

Meter signatures are not necessary for the first reading experiences, though they can be notated on the reading examples along with bar lines. If the students know what note value equals a "ta" or count, then they can read patterns without knowing meter. Prior to learning the meaning of the meter signature, students need to experience the patterns of strong and weak beats in music. Movement exercises, such as those offered by Jaques-Dalcroze and others, are a wonderful tool for developing this understanding. For example, to establish a sense of metrical stress, have students step to the beat and bend their forward knees on the strong beats while singing in solfège. An arm movement also could accompany this bending motion to reinforce the feeling of strong and weak. Another approach is to have students keep the beat by imitating a pattern of patting on strong beats and clapping on weak beats that imitates the down–up feel of the stress, such as pat–clap for duple and pat–clap–clap for triple. Teachers should offer exercises in both duple and triple meters from the very beginning to help students experience these two basic pulse groupings.

As students become comfortable showing strong and weak beats in their movements and their singing, they can derive the meter signature from this experience. Counting is probably the easiest means of introducing meter. By counting 1 on every strong beat and adding numbers to the intervening beats they can come up with the top number of the meter signature. For example, the $\frac{3}{4}$ pattern of S–W–W | S–W–W or *pat–clap–clap* | *pat*–clap–clap yields *1–2–3* | *1–2–3*. If students can think of metrical relationships and their subdivisions as simply variations on duple and triple stress combinations, then the connection between the meter signature and the sound of the rhythm becomes very evident.

Once meter signatures are introduced, it is important to establish the independence of the quarter note and the "beat." To help foster this independence and demonstrate the function of the bottom number in the meter signature, take familiar pieces and/or patterns and notate them in different meters, as shown in example 4.1.

EXAMPLE 4.1. NOTATING DIFFERENT METERS.

EXAMPLE 4.2. "SIMPLE GIFTS" REBARRED WITHOUT A PICKUP.

Another game to play with meter is to rebar a melody by moving the bar line over one beat and read it again to experience the changes that metrical stress can bring to a piece. Example 4.2 shows the familiar melody of "Simple Gifts" rebarred without the pickup note.

Teaching Note Names

Students do not need to know the names of the notes in order to sight-sing in a relative solmization system. This may seem strange, but they really only need the location of "do" or "1." From there they can find the other scale steps by their location on the staff and sound them out. Early on, a teacher can identify the note name for "do" as they place it on the staff, such as pointing to the first space in treble clef and saying, "For this piece, f is 'do,'" without offering further explanation. Eventually note names are important for identifying key signatures so that students can find their own "do" and for connecting solfège to performance on an instrument such as the piano.

When a teacher is introducing the note names, several materials are helpful. The typical mnemonics for the lines and spaces, such as Every Good Boy Does Fine and FACE, are fine, but they require an extra step to be translated. In order to be functional, however, note names eventually need to be memorized. One of the best ways to achieve memorization is through drill and practice. Two visuals can be helpful in drilling note names:

1. A combination piano keyboard/grand staff as shown in figure 4.4 provides a compact but complete reference for pitch names. This has the advantage of tying note names to the sounds on the piano and of offering treble and bass clef simultaneously. A teacher could drill students using either the keyboard or the staff to test their knowledge.
2. Another visual aid that is more portable is the "hand staff." The teacher holds up his or her left hand with the palm inward and

FIGURE 4.4. THE PIANO KEYBOARD AND THE GRAND STAFF.

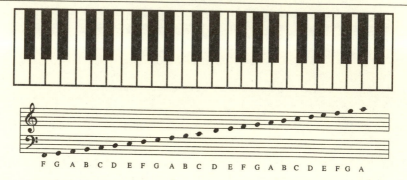

fingers facing right to provide a model of the five lines (fingers) and spaces of the staff. Then the teacher uses the right index finger to point to various locations on the left hand in order to drill students on note names (fig.4.5). The teacher should always specify treble or bass clef and alternate frequently, so that students are encouraged to learn the position of notes in both clefs from the very beginning. It is also helpful for students to learn that treble and bass clef are also known as G and F clef, respectively. By showing them how the bottom of the treble clef circles g and the dots of the bass clef highlight f, the teacher alerts them to a consistent reference note in each clef.

Ultimately, students should have note names memorized so that their recall becomes automatic. Timed tests are one of the best ways to ensure this kind of drill learning, and they can be a fun challenge for the students. With a grand staff on the board, the teacher points to various locations at 30-second intervals while the students write the names of the notes identified, gradually reducing the time interval to 5 seconds between notes.

FIGURE 4.5. DRAWING OF THE "HAND STAFF."

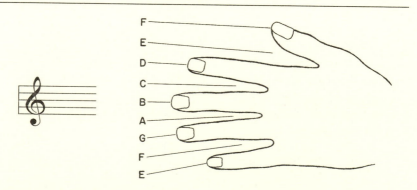

Teaching Key Signatures

Some teachers present key signatures simply by writing the circle of fifths on the board and drilling until it is learned. Recall of key signatures, like that of note names, eventually should be automatic in order to be truly functional. However, the straight drill approach has some disadvantages. First of all, it is daunting to the student who has perhaps just learned note names to try to memorize which altered notes of what type relate to which key. Second, it does not give the student any information about *why* key signatures are necessary.

The reason students need to know key signatures is so that they can find "do" or "1," so it is helpful to teach students the relationship between the key signature and the major scale. If students are using fixed "do," then the key signatures are built into their reading as they learn which syllables to alter for fa major or sol major. Building a major scale, using the sequence demonstrated in figure 4.6, teaches students that the altered notes are necessary in order to maintain the familiar sound of the major scale. Students need not learn all key signatures at once, but using this approach they could discover the key signature for a major key built on any note.

FIGURE 4.6. LESSON SEQUENCE FOR BUILDING A MAJOR SCALE.

Material
Piano positioned with the keys facing the choir. Worksheets shown below with staff lines. Students must be familiar with note names in treble and bass clefs.

1. Students have a worksheet that looks like this:

2. Teacher has students sing the C major scale on solfège.
3. Teacher   "Let's see what that looks like on the staff."
      Teacher then plays each note of the C scale as notated on the sheet and asks if it belongs in a major scale. Students may sing along on solfège.
NOTE: The teacher may be able to skip this step if students know that C major is all the white keys from c to c, but it doesn't hurt to review.
4. Teacher   "Now let's sing a different major scale. Let's sing the E major scale."
      Teacher gives e as "do" and students sing the E major scale on solfège.

→

FIGURE 4.6. continued

> Teacher "Does it sound the same?"
> Students "Yes."
5. Teacher "Now we're going to build a major scale starting on e. Do you think anything will change? . . . What? . . . Let's build scale 2 which starts on e."

Sequence

a) Students write in notes on all the lines and spaces up through the next e.
b) Students write the letter names below each note.
c) Teacher starts on e and plays the next *notated* pitch (f natural) and asks students if it fits in the scale.

6. Teacher "Does this note [f ♮] sound like it fits in the E major scale?"
> Students "No."
> Teacher "How about this one? (plays f♯)"
> Students "Yes."
> Teacher "How would you write that note? Remember this is 're' so it still needs to be on the adjacent space."
> Students "Add a sharp."

7. Teacher "Let's keep going." (Teacher starts on e again and plays e–f♯–g.) "Does this note (g) fit in the major scale?"
> Students "No."

8. Teacher proceeds through the entire scale in this way with students using their ears to build a scale that is notated like this:

Example 2

NOTE: The sequence in step 5 keeps students from notating e–g♭–a♭ instead of e–f♯–g♯ because all of the note names are in place before the scale building begins. The same process can be used to build keys on any pitch and in any clef. A final step to transition to key signatures follows.

Transition to Key Signatures

9. Teacher gives the students a notated copy of a familiar melody such as "My Country 'tis of Thee" in C major, and asks them to rewrite it in E major using their worksheet:

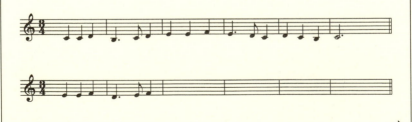

→

FIGURE 4.6. continued

10. Teacher plays the rewritten melody without accidentals and asks students what needs to be added.
11. Students then add in all the sharps for E major. When they think they're done, the teacher checks it by playing what they've notated so that they can listen and evaluate their work.
12. Teacher can then explain that key signatures are a kind of musical shorthand to keep from having to write in all the accidentals (sharps in this case). Referring to the E major scale they built, teacher asks them how many sharps are in E major. Instead of writing in *every* f♯, they can "move" f♯ over to the far right. This tells the person playing or singing that all f's are sharped for this piece.

Students who use relative solmization can already transpose sung melodies easily by moving "do" to a different note. The key signature is a shortcut that students begin to appreciate if they have to also transpose the written melody to a different key and write in all the accidentals. After students have "built" several keys it is interesting to have them put the key signatures in order, based on the number of accidentals, and see if any patterns emerge.

Eventually, memorization is the most desirable way to learn the key signatures, but there is a useful trick that can help students figure out the key from the key signature without memorization. In both sharp and flat keys, students can use the last accidental in the key signature to point them to the correct key. For sharp keys students can always find "do" by going up one line or space from the last sharp. However, one thing that confuses students is that some sharp keys are labeled by just the note name, like G or D, while others are called F♯ or C♯. To them, it would make more sense to call all the sharp keys _ -sharp. By going up one line or space from the last sharp they learn the note name of the key, but there is one more step. They must check the key signature to see if *that* note has been altered; if not, then the key is called by the note name without a sharp. For example, in figure 4.7 the first two key signatures can be calculated by using the "last sharp" method. Students might come back with the answers D and F. At that point, the teacher asks them to go back and check the key signature for altered pitches.

For flat keys, students can always find "do" by going down four lines and spaces from the last flat. The last flat is counted as "4," and then the students count down (4–3–2–1). Try this system for the flat keys in figure 4.7. Again, students check the key signature to see if the note has been altered before naming the key. Since almost all the flat keys are called _ -flat, an easier trick is to simply go to the second to last flat to find "do"; of course this does not work for F major.

FIGURE 4.7. HANDOUT ON IDENTIFYING MAJOR KEY SIGNATURES.

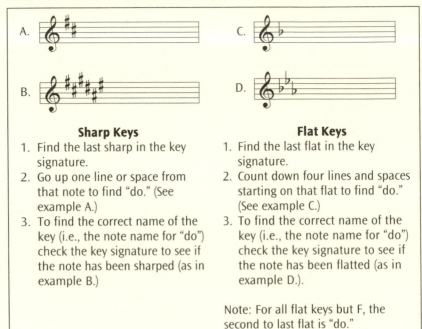

Sharp Keys	Flat Keys
1. Find the last sharp in the key signature.	1. Find the last flat in the key signature.
2. Go up one line or space from that note to find "do." (See example A.)	2. Count down four lines and spaces starting on that flat to find "do." (See example C.)
3. To find the correct name of the key (i.e., the note name for "do") check the key signature to see if the note has been sharped (as in example B.)	3. To find the correct name of the key (i.e., the note name for "do") check the key signature to see if the note has been flatted (as in example D.).
	Note: For all flat keys but F, the second to last flat is "do."

Once students have learned several key signatures, they can begin to learn that these signatures stand for more than one key. This is where minor "la" or minor "6" is helpful in illustrating the relationship between major and minor scales. Students must learn that when identifying keys for sight-singing they have to look not only at the key signature but also at the starting and ending pitches and other accidentals. The lesson in figure 4.11 will provide an example of a sequential approach to identifying and singing in a minor key.

These are just a few examples of how to introduce music fundamentals to a choir. The most important point to remember is that students can sing many things by sound even before they learn what all the symbols mean and their sense of sound can guide them to a deeper understanding of music fundamentals.

SINGLE-LINE SIGHT-SINGING

As students become familiar with some basic pitch and rhythm patterns and learn how to identify certain key and meter signatures, they need to be taught a consistent procedure for approaching a new piece of music. Unlike in the prenotational lessons, the students are now required to identify which note is "do" or "1," how many beats are in a measure, what note value receives one beat, and patterns in the pitches or rhythms of a melody that are problematic. By teaching students a consistent music-reading sequence the teacher ensures that they seek out the necessary information given in the notation to help them read the melody successfully. In addition, learning this procedure fosters an independence from the need for director instructions. Four music-reading lesson models are presented here, one a beginning level, the second and third slightly more advanced, and a fourth lesson that introduces another level of complexity.

The purpose of these lessons is not only to practice sight-singing but also to teach students what to look for when reading a melody. When asking students to identify different aspects of the score such as the meter and key, it is often helpful to have them explain how they got the answer. For example, in step 7 of figure 4.8 where the student identifies the key as B-flat major, the teacher asks how they know that it is major. The student might have been asked how they figured out the key from the key signature. This helps students who may not have gotten the same answer or had no clue how to find that piece of information.

The example given in figure 4.8 is rather elementary in terms of the number of questions supplied by the teacher and the "practicing" of cer-

FIGURE 4.8. A BEGINNING-LEVEL MUSIC-READING PROCEDURE.

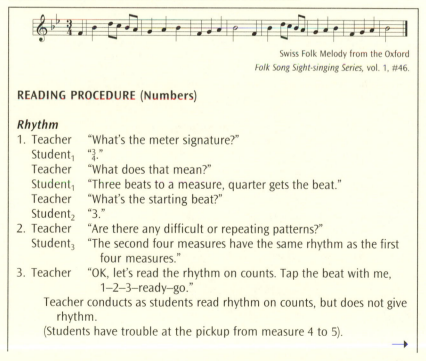

Swiss Folk Melody from the Oxford
Folk Song Sight-singing Series, vol. 1, #46.

READING PROCEDURE (Numbers)

Rhythm
1. Teacher   "What's the meter signature?"
   Student₁   "$\frac{3}{4}$."
   Teacher   "What does that mean?"
   Student₁   "Three beats to a measure, quarter gets the beat."
   Teacher   "What's the starting beat?"
   Student₂   "3."
2. Teacher   "Are there any difficult or repeating patterns?"
   Student₃   "The second four measures have the same rhythm as the first four measures."
3. Teacher   "OK, let's read the rhythm on counts. Tap the beat with me, 1–2–3–ready–go."
   Teacher conducts as students read rhythm on counts, but does not give rhythm.
   (Students have trouble at the pickup from measure 4 to 5).

→

FIGURE 4.8. continued

Evaluate

4. Teacher   "Any problems?"
   Student₄   "We missed the pickup in measure 4."
   Teacher   "OK. We need to make sure that beat 3 in measure 4 leads to beat 1 in measure 5."
5. Teacher   "Start right on beat 3 in measure 4. Tap the beat with me, 1–2–3–ready–go."
   Teacher conducts as students read rhythm on counts, but does not give rhythm.

   3   1   2 & 3 &   1 2 3

6. Teacher   "Good. Let's count the whole thing again from the beginning."
   Students read on counts.

Pitch

7. Teacher   "What's the key signature?"
   Student₅   "B-flat major."
   Teacher   "How do we check to see if it's in a major key?"
   Student₅   "Starting and ending note. It starts on F and ends on B-flat."
   Teacher   "What scale step numbers are those in B-flat?"
   Student₆   "5 and 1."
8. Teacher   "Let's sing the B-flat major scale." (Students sing.)
               "Look through and see if you find any difficult or repeating patterns." (Gives time to study.)
   Teacher   "Now let's speak through the melody on scale steps in rhythm."
   Teacher sets slower tempo, students tap beat and speak numbers.

Evaluate

9. Teacher   "Where are the repeating patterns?"
   Student₇   "The second four measures are a repeat of the first just like the rhythm."
   Teacher   "Good. Any potential problem patterns?"
   Student₈   "The first three notes might be hard and also the pattern from measure 2 to 3."
10. Teacher   "OK. Look over those spots. Where's 1?"
    Students sing, teacher corrects if necessary. Teacher points to
    1–3–5–3–1–5₁–1 on board as students sing on numbers.
    Option: Teacher takes them through the following patterns:
               1) 5₁–1–3–2–1   2) 1–6₁–7₁–1–5₁–6₁–7₁–1

Reading 1

11. Teacher   "Tune up in B-flat" (Students sing 1–3–5–3–1–5₁–1.)
    Teacher sets slow tempo, students tap the beat and sing on numbers.

Evaluate

12. Teacher   "Any problem spots?"

→

FIGURE 4.8. continued

NOTE: At this point, the teacher can actually work on individual measures for either pitch or rhythm, reviewing previous steps as necessary, and can emphasize strategies regarding repeated patterns or sequences. The teacher should also emphasize the need for phrasing and dynamics.

Reading 2
13. Teacher   "Where is 1?"
    Students sing and then tune up in B-flat again by singing:
    1–3–5–3–1–5₁–1.
    Teacher   "Where is starting pitch?"
    Students sing the starting pitch. Teacher sets tempo and conducts.
    Students sing through on scale numbers in rhythm.

tain patterns before reading, but it teaches students to look ahead for both difficult and repeating rhythm and pitch patterns. It also teaches them to establish the rhythmic shape first, before reading pitch. This can prevent a common problem with some singers who often approach sight-reading as an exercise in pitch reading only and ignore the rhythmic values of the notes. The opposite problem can also occur. If singers do not have a clear sense of the rhythmic shape of a melody, they can actually make pitch errors because they are focusing on singing the correct rhythm. To make this procedure more advanced the teacher need only remove some of the steps in the sequence prior to having the students read. Figure 4.9 shows the same lesson but in a slightly more advanced form.

The amount of support the teacher provides depends on the level of the students and on the difficulty of the melody. The preceding lesson

FIGURE 4.9. AN INTERMEDIATE SIGHT-SINGING PROCEDURE.

Swiss Folk Melody from the Oxford
Folk Song Sight-singing Series, vol. 1, #46.

READING PROCEDURE (Numbers)

Rhythm
1. Teacher   "Look through the piece and identify the meter and starting beat and any difficult or repeating patterns."
    Give students time to study.
2. Teacher   "OK. let's read the rhythm on counts. Tap the beat with me, 1–2–3–ready–go"
    Teacher conducts but does not give rhythm while students read rhythm on counts.

→

FIGURE 4.9. continued

Evaluate
3. Teacher   "Take a moment to review any problem spots."
      Give students time to look through.
4. Teacher   "OK. Let's count through just from the pickup to measure 5 [if
                  necessary]."
      Teacher conducts while students read rhythm on counts.

Pitch
5. Teacher   "Look through and identify the key and starting scale step."
      Give students time to study.
   Teacher   "What scale step number do we start on?"
   Student$_1$ "5."
6. Teacher   "Look through and see if you find any difficult or repeating
                  patterns."
      Give students time to study then have them sing 1–3–5–3–1–5$_|$–1 in
         B-flat.
7. Teacher   "Let's speak through on scale steps in rhythm."
      Teacher sets slow tempo, students tap the beat and chant on numbers.

Evaluate
8. Teacher   "Take a moment to review any problem spots."
      Give students time to look through. Tune up in B-flat: 1–3–5–3–1–5$_|$–1.

Reading 1
9. Teacher sets slow tempo, students tap the beat and sing on numbers.

Evaluate
10. Teacher   "Any problem spots?"
NOTE: At this point, the teacher can again work on individual
measures for either pitch or rhythm, reviewing previous steps as necessary.
Ask the students for suggestions on how to approach difficult spots.
Emphasize the need for phrasing and dynamics.

Reading 2
11. Teacher   "Where is 1?"   (Students sing scale step 1.)
                  "Where is the starting pitch?"   (Students sing scale step 5.)
      Teacher sets tempo and conducts. Students sing through on
         numbers in rhythm.

could be made even more advanced by skipping the step of speaking through the melody on rhythm syllables. If the rhythm is not too challenging for the students, they can speak through it the first time on the pitch syllables in preparation for singing through. As more complex melodies are introduced, the teacher can increase the number of steps in the sequence to help the students be successful. When working on easier melodies the teacher can move to a procedure that relies even more on the students' own preparation, such as the example in figure 4.10. For

FIGURE 4.10. THE STUDY APPROACH.

German Folk Melody from the Oxford
Folk Song Sight-singing Series, vol. 1, #44.

READING PROCEDURE (Movable "do")
1. Break students into groups of three. Give them 45 seconds to study the melody.
2. Have students identify the meter signature, the key (and tonality), the starting syllable. Can they identify any repeating patterns?

Reading 1
3. Teacher gives pitch and students sing d–m–s–m–d–s₁–d in G major. Teacher sets moderate to slow tempo.
   Students tap the beat and sing through the melody on solfège in rhythm.

Evaluate
4. Teacher   "What do we need to watch out for on the next reading?"
   Teacher might suggest that students try to show more of the phrasing and the dynamics throughout.

Reading 2
5. Teacher has students sing "do" (replay g if necessary) and then has them sing the starting pitch (d).
   Teacher sets tempo and conducts as students sing through on solfège in rhythm.

this lesson, the emphasis is on cooperative learning and individual study prior to group reading. Notice that all three procedures mention the need for expressive elements such as phrasing and dynamics and all three give the students at least two opportunities to read through the melody.

Introducing Minor

Figure 4.11 shows how the beginning music-reading procedure can be used when encountering musical material that is more difficult or less familiar: in this case a first encounter with minor tonality. This example uses the syllable system of movable "do" with minor "la" to show the ease of introducing minor this way. Since a new pitch-reading element

FIGURE 4.11. BEGINNING SIGHT-SINGING PROCEDURE: INTRODUCING MINOR.

READING PROCEDURE (Movable "do"/minor "la")

Rhythm

1. Teacher   "What's the meter signature?"
 Student₁   "$\frac{4}{4}$."
 Teacher   "What does that mean?"
 Student₁   "Four beats to a measure, quarter note gets the beat."
 Teacher   "What's the starting beat?"
 Student₂   "One."
2. Teacher   "Are there any difficult or repeating patterns?"
 Student₃   "Measure 2 has an off beat."
 Teacher   "Right, we call that a syncopated rhythm. Let's read that measure."
     Students tap the beat with teacher and read "ti–ta–ta–a–a."
     (Correct as needed.)
 Teacher   "Does that rhythm appear anywhere else?"
 Student₄   "Measure 3, and then partly in measures 4 and 6."
     Students tap the beat with teacher and read the rhythms in measures 4 and 6.
     (Correct as needed.)
3. Teacher   "Let's read the whole rhythm on 'ta–ti.' Tap the beat with me, 'ta–ta–rea–dy go.'"   ("rea–dy go" = "ti–ti ta")
     Teacher conducts as students chant on "tas and tis."

Pitch

4. Teacher   "What's the key signature?"
 Student₅   "G major."
 Teacher   "How do we check to see if it is major?"
 Student₅   "Starting and ending notes, which are e and e."
5. Teacher   "What solfège syllable is e in G major?"
 Student₆   "La."
 Teacher   "What does that suggest to you?"
 Student₆   "Minor?"
 Teacher   "Yes, e minor."
6. Teacher   "Another way to check if a melody is in a minor key is to look for any altered notes or accidentals. In minor the leading tone, which is 'sol,' might be raised. Are there any accidentals in this melody?"
 Student₇   "Yes. There's a d#."

→

78

FIGURE 4.11. continued

> Teacher   "How would we sing that syllable?"
> Student₇   "Change it from 'sol' to 'si'."
> Teacher   "Right. That makes it a half step from 'la' like a leading tone."
> 7. Teacher   "Let's sing the e minor scale with the raised syllable 'si.'"
>   "What's the starting syllable?"
> Student₈   "La."
>   Students sing the e minor scale on solfège with the raised leading tone.
> 8. Teacher   "Good. Let's speak through the melody in rhythm using solfège syllables."
>   Teacher sets slower tempo as students tap beat and chant solfège.

Evaluate
> 9. Teacher   "Are there repeating pitch patterns?"
> Student₉   "Yes. Measures 1 and 5 are the same, and 2 and 6 are similar."
> Teacher   "Good. Any potential problem patterns?"
> Student₁₀   "Measure 4."
>   Teacher has students speak that measure alone to get the solfège with the rhythm.
> 10. Teacher   "Where's la?" (Students sing "la"; teacher replays e if necessary)
>   Teacher points to l–d–m–d–l–si–l on board as students sing.
>   **Option:** Teacher takes them through the following patterns:

>   1) l–si–l–t–d–t–d–r–m   2) m–m–d–r–m–d–l

Reading 1
> 11. Teacher sets slow tempo, students tap the beat and sing the melody on solfège.

Evaluate
> 12. Teacher   "Any problem spots?"
> **NOTE:** At this point, the teacher can actually work on individual measures for either pitch or rhythm, reviewing previous steps as necessary. For example:

Reading 2
> 13. Teacher   "Where is la?" (Students sing "la"; teacher replays e if necessary.) "Sing the e minor scale and tonic triad." (Students sing.)
> Teacher   "Where is starting pitch?" (Students sing "la.")
> Teacher   "This time, try to pay attention to the dynamics as you sing through."
>   Teacher sets tempo and conducts as students sing on solfège in rhythm.

is being introduced, a melody with repetitive rhythm has been chosen, so the rhythm-reading sequence is more rapid. Following the lesson, alternate procedures for minor "do" and fixed "do" are discussed.

Did you recognize the melody? Using familiar melodies that the students can discover as they read helps them to practice unfamiliar syllable combinations by providing a familiar framework. As this example illustrates, there is no reason for teachers to delay introducing minor to their students. It is simply a variation on a theme that is already established in the music-reading procedure. By identifying the key signature using the questioning procedure illustrated in figure 4.11, the teacher reinforces the fact that different tonalities can share the same key signature. A mistake that even college students can make when sight-singing is not looking ahead before they start reading and thus assuming the melody is in a major key. Minor "la" makes the transition to reading minor much easier because it illustrates the relative relationship very naturally. This is especially useful in melodies that modulate between the major and minor tonics.

If a teacher is using fixed "do," the minor tonality will happen almost by default as the student reads through the piece with the necessary altered syllable. The teacher can help students by pointing out that certain accidentals that are not part of the key signature may indicate a minor melody. Having students realize that the starting and ending pitches do not match up with the major scale will also make reading easier. In the Dalcroze method, students are asked to sing scales that start on any note of the C major scale, thus producing the different modes, including minor. Students who use fixed "do" still need to recognize the sounds of the different tonalities in order to read them effectively. Having students tune up on the scale beginning with the minor tonic will set a harmonic context that will aid them in reading the melody.

Minor "do" requires that the student identify the key as minor and then set the minor tonic as "do" with altered syllables. While this seems less efficient than using minor "la," it does have the advantage of reinforcing the connection between the syllable "do" and the tonic of a key. One of the difficulties of reading in minor "la" is the feeling of coming to rest harmonically on a syllable other than "do." Students will sometimes inadvertently shift "la" to "do" in response to this sense of minor tonic.

The Song-Learning Procedure

All of the lessons presented thus far, while different in difficulty level and material, share an underlying structure. It is this structure that students need to learn in order to become independent music readers. Figure 4.12 outlines the "song-learning procedure" that forms the basis for the sight-singing lessons. Reinforcing this procedure through a variety of differ-

FIGURE 4.12. OUTLINE OF THE SONG-LEARNING PROCEDURE.

Song Learning Procedure
1. Rhythm
    a) Identify the meter and starting beat.
    b) Scan for difficult and repeating patterns.
    c) Set a steady tempo and chant the rhythm while keeping the beat.
    d) Evaluate.
2. Pitch
    a) Identify the key signature, tonality, and starting syllable.
    b) Scan for difficult and repeating patterns.
    c) Establish sense of key through tuning up; perhaps sing difficult patterns.
    d) Set a steady tempo and chant or sing solfège (or other syllables) in rhythm.
    e) Evaluate.

ent lessons will help students to approach reading a new piece of music in a consistent and logical way. It is also helpful to teach students the steps of the procedure directly so that they become aware of the underlying structure in their lessons.

MULTIPART SIGHT-SINGING

While single-line melodies provide the best introduction to the challenges of sight-singing, the eventual goal is to apply this knowledge to reading both solo and group literature. The use of canons to introduce multipart singing is an outstanding transition from single-line melodies, especially for students who are less experienced singing in parts. However, the canon approach is best used when the different voice parts have similar ranges, as in a treble choir. Middle school singers, especially boys, have very different ranges as their voices change. For these singers, a canon is the last thing a director wants, because the different voice parts have very different registers. Pieces with four-part harmony, in limited but different ranges, are better choices for sight-singing material at this level. Another benefit of using four-part material is that each voice part has its own quirks of harmony and voice leading in a homophonic texture to which choral singers must become accustomed. Sopranos are often surprised at the amount of skipping around that the bass part normally does. Consequently, simultaneous multipart sight-reading is a skill that must be taught in addition to single-part sight-reading. With the proper materials it is relatively easy to transfer the song-learning sequence of the single-line melody to multipart sight-singing, as shown in figure 4.13.

FIGURE 4.13. MULTIPART SIGHT-SINGING LESSON PLAN 1.

READING PROCEDURE (Fixed "do")

Rhythm
1. Teacher has students look through the piece and identify the meter.
2. Teacher sets tempo and conducts and students tap the beat while chanting through the rhythm on "ta–ti."

Evaluate
3. Teacher reviews and discusses any problem spots with students. Students chant rhythm for any problem measures, either with all four parts or all on an individual part.

Pitch
4. Teacher has students look through the piece and identify the key signature and which solfège syllables must be altered for that key. For example: For a piece in E-flat major, "ti" becomes "teh", "mi" becomes "meh", "la" becomes "leh."
5. Students sing the E-flat major scale on solfège with altered syllables, and then sing the tonic triad in E-flat: "meh–sol–teh–sol–meh."
6. Teacher has students look through and see if they find any difficult or repeating patterns. (Give time to study.)
7. Teacher asks individuals in each section to identify their starting syllable and then all students speak through on solfège in rhythm while tapping the beat.

Evaluate
8. Teacher takes a moment to review any problem spots.

Reading 1
9. Teacher has the choir sing the tonic again (can check with piano), then the tonic triad (meh–sol–the–sol–meh). Then each section sings their starting pitch on the syllable (can double on piano if needed).
10. Teacher sets a slow tempo, students tap the beat and sing on solfège.
Optional: Piano doubling the first time through with soft pedal.

→

FIGURE 4.13. continued

> **Evaluate**
> 11. At this point, the teacher can actually work on individual measures for either pitch or rhythm, reviewing previous steps as necessary. Ask the students for suggestions on how to approach difficult spots.
>
> *Reading 2*
> 12. Teacher has the choir sing "meh" again (can check with piano),and then each section sings their starting pitch on the syllable (can double on piano if needed). Teacher might ask students to pay more attention to musical elements such as phrasing, dynamics, tone, etc.
> 13. Teacher sets a slow tempo, students tap the beat and sing on solfège.
>
> *Evaluate*
> 14. Teacher reviews and emphasizes musical features or persistently difficult passages.
>
> *Reading 3*
> 15. Teacher conducts while the choir sings through on text working for as musical a performance as possible.

The similarities of this sequence to the single-line procedure are evident, but there are some important differences. The first is the need to identify rhythmic differences among different voice parts. A common source of rhythmic errors in multipart reading is that students all follow the rhythm of the melody (or the loudest part). Another challenge is listening for "harmonic" errors. Students may sing the right syllable but be doubling another voice part inadvertently. The most common doubling is having one of the inner voices move to the melody (especially young tenors). Make sure that the sections get started on the right pitch and syllable, and use patterns from different voice parts to tune up in the key. After identifying problems in the first reading, all of the students can be asked to sing a difficult pattern that occurs in one voice part. This helps the voice part and provides good reading practice for all of the singers, especially when they have to read in unfamiliar clefs.

The lesson plan in figure 4.13 uses fixed "do" as the pitch-reading system. The primary difference between fixed and movable "do" is in the way in which the key is established. In fixed "do," instead of using the key signature to find "do," it is used to identify the altered syllables and the starting note of the scale. The key is not E-flat major but "mi"-flat or "meh" major. This tells the students what they must know about the syllables needed to sing the scale. Other aspects of the reading procedure remain unchanged.

FIGURE 4.14. MULTI-PART SIGHT-SINGING LESSON PLAN 2.

"Cast Thy Burden upon the Lord" — Mendelssohn

READING PROCEDURE (Movable "do")

1. Teacher plays the tonic triad (broken form) and gives students 45 seconds to study the piece.
2. Students are asked to identify and discuss any potential problem spots — for example, identifying any large leaps in the voice leading.
3. Teacher plays the tonic triad again and conducts as students speak through the piece on solfège in rhythm while tapping the beat.
4. Students get 30 seconds to review what they just read and discuss mistakes.

Reading 1

5. Teacher plays the tonic triad (broken form) and has students sing their starting pitches together on solfège.
6. Teacher sets a moderate to slow tempo. Students tap the beat and sing through on solfège in rhythm.

Evaluate

7. Students review problem spots before next reading.

Reading 2

8. Teacher has students sing "do" (reset if necessary) and then has them sing their starting pitch.
9. Teacher sets tempo and conducts as students sing through on text.

A more advanced multipart procedure would encourage the students to try to anticipate problem spots before they read and evaluate their own performance afterward. The procedure given in figure 4.14 is similar to sight-singing procedures used in choral contests. The main difference is that students can discuss features of the melody but do not get to sing it out loud until they read it the first time.

Notice that in all of the lessons presented thus far students are always asked to keep the beat while they chant or sing. Having some movement accompany the beat reinforces the importance of rhythmic awareness

FIGURE 4.15. SAMPLE "HANDS" FOR THE SOLFÈGE CARD GAME.

and helps keep them from stopping when they run into trouble. One can see how this sequence could easily be used in rehearsal for the first read-through of a piece of literature. This is the goal of multipart sight-singing: to be able to apply the skills to reading new literature in rehearsal.

SIGHT-SINGING GAMES

Establishing a consistent procedure for music reading is an important goal of sight-singing instruction, but so is having fun. Sometimes the drill and repetition required for skill building can be presented in the form of a game. The following games are examples of how very difficult skills can be presented as a fun challenge to students. The activities build inner hearing, sense of key, rhythm-reading skills, aural skills, and solfège pattern recognition. These games should not be done in lieu of sequential instruction but in addition to it.

A Solfège Card Game

One of the best tools for practicing sight-singing is a deck of cards. Take a normal deck of cards and remove all of the face cards and the 9s and 10s, leaving ace through 8 in every suit. The melodies are read with aces as "do" or "1" and on up the scale and can be read on numbers or solfège. Shuffle the deck and then "deal" the cards faceup in any number you wish. The students must sing the pattern they are dealt either individually or in a group. In order to ensure more singable melodies, it is often a good idea to stack the deck a bit by removing most of the cards for certain scale degrees. For example, a good deck for beginning sight-singing practice might contain four aces, one 2 card, two 3 cards, one 4, three 5s, one 6, one 7, and four 8s. Another way to ensure readability is to begin and end the melodies on an ace, 5, or 8. Figure 4.15 illustrates the pitch patterns that result from two "hands" dealt from this deck. For an added challenge the cards could be laid over a rhythm pattern such as | | | ⊓| ⊓⊔, with one card for each note value.

"Name That Tune"

Another fun way to practice use of solfège or hand signs is to play "Name That Tune." The teacher notates a pitch pattern in solfège on the board or overhead and then covers it. Students can compete individually or in teams to "name that tune" from the solfège. This is a good way to begin a sight-singing lesson because it gets students focused on reading solfège. The melodies can be notated in a variety of ways: solfège, actual notation, or hand signs (fig. 4.16). Students are not allowed to sing what they see out loud; they must come up with it internally. If the teacher wants to make this more like the real game, students can be given a clue as to the melody title and then bid for how little of the melody they need to see in order to guess.

FIGURE 4.16. "NAME THAT TUNE."

"Name That Tune"
This game can be organized a number of ways. One way is to notate the tune on the board. The teacher can then uncover the tune and call on the first person who raises their hand.

The same tune could be notated using only solfège syllables with no rhythm:

d d r m d m r d d r m r t

or stick notation:

d d r m d m r d d r m r t

Another approach, which is more like the original game, is to have students "bid" for how many notes they need in order to name the tune. Then give them the hand signs in rhythm for however many notes they bid.

Bingo #1

A fun and challenging form of dictation is to play the game bingo where students are handed cards with short solfège patterns written in each box (fig. 4.17). The teacher sets a key and has the students tune up in the key. The teacher then calls out a letter and plays on the piano or sings on neutral syllables one of the patterns. The students then look to see if that pattern is under the letter on their cards and, if so, cover it with a piece of paper. The teacher can vary the keys and the mode of presentation throughout the game to add to the challenge. Rhythm patterns can also be used as examples, as seen under letters "N" and "G" of the sample card.[1]

This game may seem very difficult (and it certainly can be), as students have to translate what they hear into solfège and then find it on the card. However, the patterns are short and the students need only look at the examples under the specific letter. The game can be made easier by lim-

FIGURE 4.17. THE BINGO EAR-TRAINING GAME.

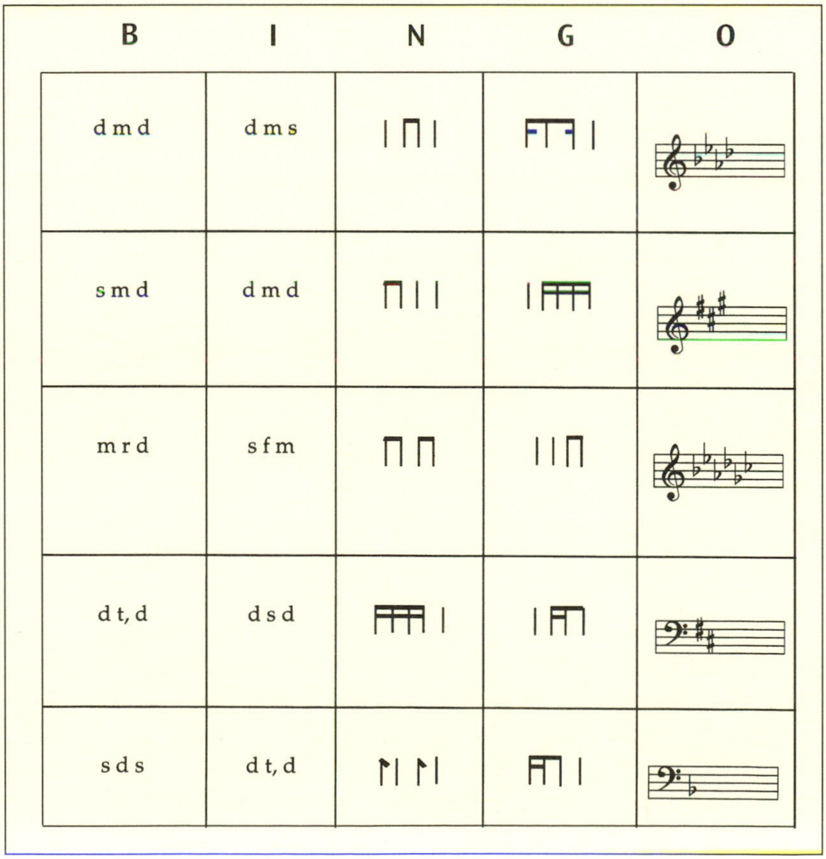

B	I	N	G	O
d m d	d m s			
s m d	d m d			
m r d	s f m			
d t, d	d s d			
s d s	d t, d			

iting the variety of patterns. That way, a simple pattern such as "d–m–d" can be used under several letters and students have fewer places to look for the necessary patterns. Another variation is to use both written and aural examples to fill in the boxes. This way students could be drilled on note names and key signatures as well as dictation. For example, the teacher could write on the board the name of a key signature, like F-sharp major or B minor, and each student would have to find it notated in a box on their card. Letter "O" of the card in figure 4.17 gives some examples for key signature practice.

Bingo #2

A second version of bingo is based not on the board game but on the song, where certain notes have to be left out or filled with claps (e.g., B-I-N-_-_). This can be done while singing a simple scale or when singing a melody or just pitch or rhythm pattern notated on the board. The idea is to designate certain notes in the pattern to be sung silently. Students then have to read the melody, leaving out the marked pitches but still maintaining the correct pitch and rhythm.[2]

This also can become a friendly competition between groups of students to see how many notes can be removed and still sung accurately. For example, if two teams started with an ascending and descending major scale, the first team would read the scale with only one pitch marked out. If they are successful, they choose the pitch to be removed for the second team, and so on.

Instant Canons

Instant canons are a tremendous ear challenge for the students and a great way to focus attention. They can be done using either pitch or rhythm. The rhythm canon is a variation on simple echo clapping. In the rhythm canon, the teacher sets a steady beat and then claps a two- or four-beat pattern for the students to echo. While the students are echoing the pattern, the teacher claps the *next* two/four beats, and so on. It is surprising how quickly students can catch onto this game and how adept they can become. One technique that can help both the students and the teacher is alternating the presentation of the rhythms from side to side so that as the students echo the pattern given on the left side, the teacher claps a new pattern on the right side. A variation of this technique involves presenting each rhythm pattern by tapping a different part of the body and then having students echo by tapping the same places on their bodies. Both techniques help to differentiate between the rhythm being echoed and the new rhythm. Some teachers even use rhythm canons as a classroom management tool; it is a nonverbal way to bring the choir back on task and into focus. This game is a good opportunity for a student-led activity as well, though they will find it challenging.

A pitch canon can be done in a similar way, with the teacher singing a solfège pattern two to four beats ahead of the students, though pitch canons should be planned out ahead of time so that the combinations are harmonically compatible. A more challenging way to do a pitch canon is to use hand signs. The teacher sets a beat and then signs the first four notes of the canon. While students are signing and singing those four notes, the teacher signs the next four beats, and so on. The teacher can choose to model the pattern silently or while singing, depending on the level of the students. Hand signs also can be used to read in harmony if the teacher is very skilled, half the class reading the right hand and half the left.

Beyond Notation

The Dalcroze approach to sight-singing often takes a very playful approach to music reading. Dalcroze's goal was to develop students' internal sense of pitch and rhythm to the point that they could "converse" musically with ease. A few ideas from Dalcroze can be use to extend sight-singing lessons to challenge the students to go beyond what is notated.

The first game is a "fill in the blanks" activity in which any melody or pitch pattern that students are sight-reading can be read again, filling in all the notes of a leap. Obviously, each note of the melody would need to be taken out of rhythm in order to do this.

A second game is to read melodies both forward and backward, keeping both pitch and rhythm accurate. This can be surprisingly difficult. Try it with the melody in example 4.3.

These two games illustrate a more playful approach to practicing music reading while actually increasing difficulty. The teacher challenges the students' aural and creative powers to go beyond what is notated and demonstrate their understanding of musical relationships. This can be taken into other areas, such as rhythm, where different measures of a melody could be read in double time or augmentation, depending on a signal from the teacher.

Games provide an excellent tool for drilling music-reading skills while offering a fun and motivating challenge to the students. Both the teacher and the students can come up with numerous variations on the games already mentioned to provide greater variety and interest in the process of developing sight-singing skills.

EXAMPLE 4.3. FILL-IN-THE-BLANKS AND RETROGRADE READING GAMES.

SEQUENCING SIGHT-SINGING INSTRUCTION

Many of the published materials presented in chapter 8 offer musical examples that are sequenced according to difficulty. While these sequences can be very helpful, they may not always reflect the pace of your students' development. In order to build sight-singing skills, the teacher must strike a balance between gradually increasing difficulty and providing sufficient repetition. A good rule of thumb is that when introducing more complexity in one area, such as a new rhythm pattern or difficult pitch sequence, make sure the material in the other areas is familiar. For example, if a teacher wants to introduce $\frac{6}{8}$ meter, then the pitch content should be mostly stepwise so that students can concentrate on the rhythmic challenge.

Sight-singing, like any skill, requires a great deal of practice. When a teacher is sequencing sight-singing lessons, it is helpful to keep in mind the three Rs of skill building: Review, Repetition, and Reinforcement.

Review

Once new content is introduced, it must be regularly reviewed, often more than the teacher might think. This is true for new musical material and more advanced reading procedures, as well as for material that has not been covered recently. New teachers often make the mistake of assuming that once a new skill has been presented and successfully demonstrated in one class period, then students "have it" and do not need to review it in the next class period. Review can take many forms. Sometimes it is just a verbal reminder to students about what was covered the day before, sometimes speaking or singing through a new pitch or rhythm sequence again before reading a different melody, and sometimes in the form of questions that highlight a reoccurrence of a particular musical element. If students have read a minor melody for the first time the day before, the teacher cannot present a new minor melody the next day and expect all aspects of the previous day's lesson to be remembered and applied to the new melody. Students will need a great deal of practice before recognition and performance of even the simplest minor solfège become ingrained.

Repetition

Repetition relates to review in terms of the need for going over information that has been previously covered, but it also relates to the way in which skills are built. When students learn a new rhythm, for instance, they will not automatically transfer the sound of that pattern to different melodies that contain it even if you review the sound of the pattern. It would seem as though once students could accurately perform a rhythm pattern in one song, they would be able to recognize it in different melodies and recall the sound. However, that is not the case. Many aspects of context, such as pitch content, tempo, and other rhythmic aspects, can interfere with students' recognition of newly learned patterns. Students require numerous opportunities for repetition of musical material in many different contexts before they can begin to transfer what they know effectively.

Reinforcement

Teachers must constantly look for opportunities to reinforce the connection between sounds and symbols that are being learned in sight-singing. That is why teaching music reading without applying it to the rehearsal of literature can work against students' skill development. Every opportunity to point out familiar material should be taken.

Solfège and numbers are often thought of as tools for students to "sound out" music that is unfamiliar, but students first need to build the necessary sound vocabulary for these systems to be effective. A great technique is to sing already-learned songs on solfège syllables or numbers. This is similar to Kodály's approach of working from the sounds of rote songs to the reading of new material. Substituting solfège for text when singing choral literature that has already been learned and polished reinforces the sound–syllable–symbol connection. It also provides an opportunity for students to practice singing solfège musically by applying the expressive elements they have been rehearsing to a solfège context. An added benefit of this technique is that singing on solfège often improves intonation, even on learned music.

Another aspect of reinforcement is returning to simpler musical materials after students have increased their reading skills but increasing the challenge in other ways. For example, once your students are reading pieces like "Cast Thy Burden upon the Lord" (fig. 4.14) easily on solfège, then ask them to read simpler pieces on a neutral syllable or text to begin to wean them from solfège syllables.

CONCLUSION

Through review, repetition, and reinforcement, a teacher can nurture students' sight-singing skills. Beyond that, students simply need numerous opportunities to practice and be successful. For any new melody they are presenting, teachers must ask, "What's the minimum amount of support I can offer and still give the students a successful reading experience?" If students have successful sight-singing experiences, they will begin to think of themselves as "readers." This positive attitude toward music reading contributes to students' future success as much as their skill development because it makes them willing to try.

RECOMMENDED READINGS

Note: See also published sight-singing materials listed in chapter 8 for lesson models and procedures.

Henke, Herbert H. (1984). The application of Émile Jaques-Dalcroze's Solfège-rhythmique to the choral rehearsal. *Choral Journal, 24* (5), 11–14.
Phillips, K. H. (1996). Teaching singers to sight-read. *Teaching Music, 3* (6), 32–33.
Texas University Interscholastic League (UIL) Music Contest Website at: http://www.utexas.edu/admin/uil/mus/index.html http://www.utexas.edu/admin/uil/mus/rules/111.html

5

Integrating Sight-Singing into the Choral Rehearsal

"You see," he went on, "it's no use at all teaching children to sight-sing if you aren't going to allow them to exercise their skills so that they may get better and better with each practice. Some fairly enlightened choir directors practice sight-singing for five minutes. That's no good! They have to practice sight-singing all the time. That way the children have to think for themselves."

"The Choirmaster," in John Bertalot's *Five Wheels to Successful Sight-Singing*

The lesson models in chapter 4 demonstrate how sight-singing can be presented systematically to choirs at beginning and advanced levels to build essential skills. The lesson models are all designed to be presented as a separate part of the rehearsal, distinct from work on the performance literature, though the lesson material can be based on music taken from choral literature. However, it is important that a teacher's commitment to sight-singing not end at the moment that the rehearsal of the literature begins. When a 10-minute sight-singing lesson is followed by a rehearsal in which parts are pounded out on the piano, sight-singing becomes an academic exercise rather than a useful skill. However, we must acknowledge that our students' voices and musicality are often developed well beyond their musicianship skills and that there is often a wide range of reading abilities within a single ensemble. To provide literature that keeps students challenged as performers, teachers often choose music that is beyond the choir's ability to sight-read successfully. How do we deal with the challenge of incorporating reading into the rehearsal without compromising the quality of the literature we perform? Solutions to this challenge may be found in the organization of the choir program itself, the choice of literature, and the teaching approaches utilized in the rehearsal.

In choir programs that teach sight-singing consistently, the amount of rehearsal time spent on instruction is balanced with the skill level of the group. The beginning groups spend a greater percentage of time on sight-singing skills and basic theory, learning or refining particular syllable or number system and singing exercises and literature that strengthen their skills. The more advanced groups, having attained a certain level of skill, work more on applying their skills to the literature in rehearsal, with less time devoted exclusively to sight-singing exercises. Consequently, they move through the note-learning stage more quickly and on to expressive and interpretive concerns. This progress may be more accelerated if instruction begins in the elementary or middle school years.

The motivation for students in beginning groups to work on these skills stems in part from a desire to "move on." The different ensembles can be organized by grade or ability or a combination of the two. For example, in a high school that has grades 9–12, it might be helpful for all freshmen to be in the same ensemble, where certain skills are taught and expectations met. The 10–12 students could then be grouped more by ability. Those who progress rapidly might move into more select ensembles the following year, while those who need more help move into "open" groups.

One way to lessen the stigma that can be associated with less-advanced groups is to have the training groups be all-male and all-female. While this may seem idealistic given the continual problem of too few men in mixed ensembles, it can be a solution to that problem in the long term. Teaching boys and girls separately is becoming accepted practice in middle school and junior high because of the particular needs of the male changing voice and the differences in maturity and musical needs between adolescent males and females. However, similar needs also occur at the high school. By teaching boys and girls separately the teacher can better address any differences in interest and ability and create ensembles that are unique in membership and in literature rather than lesser versions of the top mixed group.

CHOICE OF LITERATURE

Choosing literature is one of the choir director's most difficult and important challenges. If we provide literature at a level that matches students' *performance* ability, we often choose pieces well beyond their *reading* ability. Consequently, part learning becomes a rote experience with little connection to the skills we purport to teach. There are several solutions to this that can enrich rather than detract from the rehearsal of literature.

One solution, more commonly found in instrumental ensembles, is to have more pieces in the choir folder than will eventually be performed. Some easier pieces can be used solely for reading challenges. Students are given the tonic chord, sing a few pitch patterns, have a short time to study the score, and then read it straight through. An example of such a piece for a beginning high school choir would be Schubert's "Heilig" (ex. 5.1).

It is also important to work with music reading versus sight-reading. Since we only *sight*-read a piece once, it is perhaps more important to concentrate on what can be improved from the first reading to the second, as well as to challenge singers to incorporate musical elements such as phrasing, dynamics, and articulation as soon as possible. A piece like "Heilig" might be chosen for reading but also could become part of a performance as the director and the students explore the many musical decisions that need to be made to perform even a simple piece. There are a number of musical issues to be addressed in "Heilig," the most notable being musical phrasing accomplished through both dynamics and the rhythmic motion of the line. Choral teachers often fall into the trap of equating challenging music with the presence of particular pitch and rhythm challenges, rather than exploring the constant challenge of performing even the simplest piece more musically.

Unison singing is a good example of this point. Vaughan Williams's beautiful unison setting of "Orpheus with his Lute" (ex. 5.2) is not only a great introductory reading challenge; it is also a wonderful tool for teaching choral tone, blend, breath control, and phrasing. A similar tech-

EXAMPLE 5.1. SCHUBERT'S "HEILIG" A SIMPLE FOUR-PART HOMOPHONIC PIECE FOR SIGHT-SINGING.

Heilig

Schubert

EXAMPLE 5.2. UNISON MELODIES FOR SIGHT-SINGING.

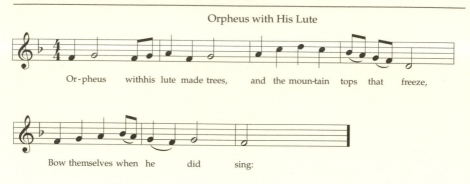

Orpheus with His Lute

Or-pheus   withhis lute made trees,   and the moun-tain tops   that   freeze,

Bow themselves when he   did   sing:

She's like the Swallow

She's like theswallow that flies so high, She's like   the ri-ver that ne-ver runs dry, She's

like   the sun - shine on the lee shore,   I   love   my love and love is no more.

nique could be used with "She's like the Swallow" (Dorian) prior to introducing either Vaughan Williams's unison setting or a choral arrangement of that melody (ex. 5.2).

Another approach would be to take a folk melody like "Shenandoah," which many students already know, and challenge them to sing it on solfège or numbers. As mentioned before, this "reverse reading" strategy can help reinforce connections between the syllable system and particular musical patterns. Singing on solfège is also effective as a tool for improving intonation after the notes have been learned. There are many wonderful arrangements of this melody that could be programmed at a later time.

There will still be times when we need to teach by rote, either because it is appropriate to the style or because the music is in a mode or meter that is beyond our singers' reading level. These instances should be looked on as opportunities to develop aural skills such as listening for repeated patterns in the music, becoming sensitive to imitating not only pitch and rhythm but also style upon first hearing, and developing a sound vocabulary regarding certain pitch and rhythm patterns. This final area can be reinforced if rote learning of a piece in $\frac{7}{8}$ or in Dorian mode can be *followed* by a reading exercise that utilizes those elements so that the sound the singers have learned connects to the symbol used to represent it.

THE CHOIR REHEARSAL

Perhaps the most difficult choice a director faces is how to introduce a new piece of music. Sometimes it can be fun to "plow through" a piece, train wrecks and all, just for the experience. Students can learn what to look for, become more astute with prereading preparation, and begin to identify patterns. This is not recommended as a strategy for beginning *every* piece, because it also can be very discouraging. When using this approach, plan the time so that students get a chance to do at least two readings, allowing the group to identify areas of improvement and show what they learned from the first reading. Perhaps one of the most important lessons students learn from this approach is how to keep the beat going and find their part in relation to it.

An alternative to the train wreck approach is reading with piano doubling. While this often leads to singers' following a fraction behind the piano, it is preferable to strict rote imitation part-by-part. One way to discourage following is to have the piano drop in and out and help with starting points or lines that are lost but never be totally present. The use of the soft pedal also can help create a more background "feel" to the keyboard, rather than the leading role it so often commands.

While the run-through approach provides a very direct connection to sight-singing training, it is not always practical or rewarding for more difficult music. In those cases, a more effective strategy is adjusting the way we teach a piece to pull out reasonable challenges as a starting point for learning. By approaching the literature structurally the director can identify important lines, harmonic progressions, or entire sections that are within the group's ability to read and use these to lead to more complex connections in the rest of the piece. Following are five examples of integrating sight-singing into the introduction and teaching of a new piece based on the structural characteristics of the music.

Folk Songs

A choral setting of a folk song, such as Pooler's "Simple Gifts," provides an opportunity for everyone in the group to sight-read the simpler folk melody before they learn their supporting part. Both the A and B parts of this melody are well within the reading abilities of many choirs. After the choir reads the melody in the soprano part on solfège or numbers, the director can add the text and work on phrasing, articulation, and diction while everyone stays on the melody. This approach not only provides a reading opportunity; it also teaches the students the musical idea on which the remainder of the piece is based, something that will help them to sing more musically. In the second verse of this arrangement (ex. 5.3), the melody alternates between the male and female voices.

After everyone has sight-read the folk melody on syllables or numbers and rehearsed on the text, this section would be a good starting point for introducing the parts. Have the students sing only when they have the melody, so that they get a feel for the necessary balance among the voice parts. Then begin to add the accompanying parts one at a time, on either solfège or text, while the other voices continue to sing only when they have the melody. Layering the parts and alternating of text and syllables make the reading challenge more accessible.

Imitative Counterpoint

Many pieces of music feature extensive points of imitation. These sections can be opportunities to provide reading challenges. A well-known

EXAMPLE 5.3. FIRST NINE MEASURES OF VERSE 2 FROM "SIMPLE GIFTS" (ARR. MARIE POOLER). COPYRIGHT 1971 (RENEWED BY G. SCHIRMER, INC.) INTERNATIONAL COPYRIGHT SECURED. ALL RIGHTS RESERVED. REPRINTED BY PERMISSION OF G. SCHIRMER, INC.

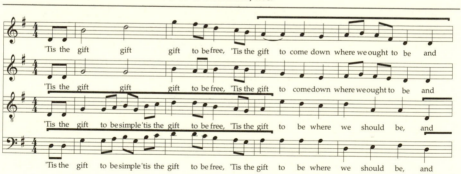

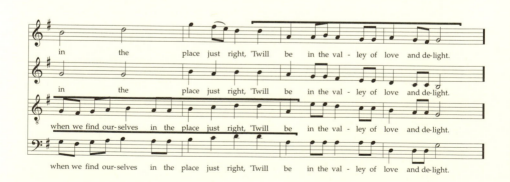

EXAMPLE 5.4. THE OPENING TENOR PART OF PALESTRINA'S "SICUT CERVUS."

do   do   re   do sol do   re mi mi fa   mi
Si -   cut cer - vus de - si - de-rat ad fon -   tes

motet like Palestrina's "Sicut cervus," with its constantly interweaving polyphony, would be daunting to read cold, but all of the sections could sight-read the opening tenor part through "fontes" (ex. 5.4). After that part has been read successfully, keep all the singers on the tenor part and move to the text to work on the diction and phrasing for this short motive with everyone in unison. This allows the teacher and the students to work on musical challenges immediately within a simplified musical context. Once that is done, have the students look for that same melody in their part. With the exception of the altos, there is fairly direct imitation through the first 20 measures. Have students read through measure 20 on their own parts, singing only where they have the melody. The other material of the opening, such as the alto imitation at the fifth and other counterpoint, can be approached as variations on the main theme. A nice way to introduce issues of balance is to have students sing the main part on the text and then introduce accompanying counterpoint on solfège or neutral syllables. While switching back and forth can be harder than reading straight through, it does make singers aware of the structural function of their line and should head off problems later on.

Another well-known example of imitative counterpoint is Passereau's "Il est bel et bon" (ex. 5.5). While the piece is in Dorian mode, the opening ritornello provides a fairly simple reading challenge. Have all students start on the soprano line, reading on syllables through measure 8, then move the altos and basses to the alto line and have them try to identify the relationship between the parts before they read it. Once these parts have been established, students will notice that the tenor and bass lines begin in close imitation with the female voices. For extra reading practice, move all sections to tenor and bass and scan the parts to identify where they differ from the soprano and alto. The use of paired imitation throughout the piece cuts the part-learning time almost in half and provides numerous "group" reading opportunities. The more intricate sections will probably require some doubling or even rote teaching to solidify.

One idea for introducing the more difficult contrasting sections of "Il est bel et bon" is to present them first as rhythm-reading challenges. Students are often able to read the rhythm of a section even when the pitch patterns are too difficult. Because of the speed of the moving lines, rhyth-

EXAMPLE 5.5. OPENING SECTION OF PASSEREAU'S "IL EST BEL ET BON."

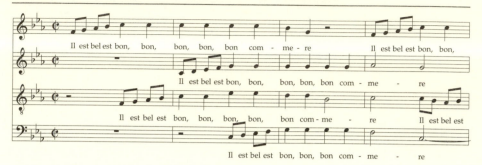

mic unity is often a problem in performances of this work. It is helpful to concentrate on rhythm alone before moving to pitch. The strategy of singing on text for the ritornello and on syllables for the new material also can provide a balance between reading challenge and satisfying musical experience.

Rote-to-Note

Much of our contemporary choral literature comes out of the world music repertoire, which seems to lend itself more to rote teaching strategies than to music reading. The pieces, while presented in published form, often come from an oral tradition, where notation is not used, and consequently many of the rhythmic and stylistic characteristics are difficult to capture in notation. These pieces can also feature challenging rhythmic and melodic figures that are not typical in Western tonal music. However, even in these pieces there can be reading opportunities. For example, the traditional Georgia Sea Islands song "Yonder Come Day" has a melodic line with a stylized rhythmic feel and some chromatic "blue" notes that could be difficult for beginning choirs to read (ex. 5.6, part II). However, the two harmony parts (parts I and III) offer very approachable reading opportunities. After students have been taught

EXAMPLE 5.6. EXCERPT FROM "YONDER COME DAY," BASED ON THE TRADITIONAL GEORGIA SEA ISLANDS SONG NEW WORDS, MUSIC AND ARRANGEMENT BY JUDITH COOK TUCKER. © 1986 JUDITH COOK TUCKER/WORLD MUSIC PRESS

the entire melody by rote (using the recommended step/clap pattern) and refined their approach to the musical style, the two harmony parts could be introduced with solfège. The solfège would help distinguish the parts from the melody and offer the students a very reasonable reading challenge.

Harmonically Based Pieces

Some homophonic pieces with simple rhythms, like the Schubert "Heilig" shown earlier, lend themselves to a four-part read-through. However, homophonic pieces also can be prepared by first singing a chord exercise that reflects certain progressions. Extracting chord progressions often works well as an introduction to reading homophonic pieces with more difficult rhythms. An example would be Ralph Johnson's arrangement of the Cameroon song "Praise the Lord!" Before introducing the more complex rhythm the teacher may wish to establish the simple harmonic flow of the piece, which repeats many times. This can be done by creating an exercise like the one in example 5.7, or by simply reading from the score chord-by-chord with the director signaling when to move.

EXAMPLE 5.7. EXCERPT OF ORIGINAL MUSIC AND HARMONIC SOLFÈGE EXERCISE FOR JOHNSON'S ARRANGEMENT OF "PRAISE THE LORD!". © 1994 BY EARTHSONGS; REPRINTED BY PERMISSION.

Original

Praise, Praise, Praise the Lord, Praise His ho - ly name al - le - lu - ia!

Harmonic Experience

Rhythmically Based Pieces

Many of the approaches discussed have emphasized pitch challenges, but what of rhythmic reading? "Praise the Lord!" provides a wonderful but difficult rhythm-reading challenge, and it may be desirable to establish the rhythm pattern prior to introducing the harmonic progression. One means of introducing complex rhythms is to first include them as a warm-up exercise. For instance, students could echo the director and hiss the following patterns as breath warm-ups (ex. 5.8). Then in the sight-singing portion of rehearsal, these patterns might come up again as a reading challenge on a single chord (ex. 5.9). While the students might not read the rhythm correctly the first time, once they hear it they will recognize it from the warm-up and learn it more quickly. By the time they actually rehearse the piece, it is a matter of identifying familiar patterns before reading through the rhythm and then re-creating them. Remember that sight-singing is a memory activity; students cannot read a pitch or rhythm pattern that they have not heard in some context before. Sight-reading

EXAMPLE 5.8. BREATH WARM-UPS BASED ON "PRAISE THE LORD!"

Breath Warmup 1

"ts"

Breath Warmup 2

"ts"

EXAMPLE 5.9. RHYTHM PRACTICE ON A CHORD WARM-UP.

"pah"

"pah"

is simply applying prior knowledge of musical patterns and relationships to novel settings.

Another great rhythm-reading tool is "count singing." If you have a piece such as Vecchi's "Io soffrirò," where the pitches are relatively easy, but the rhythm is challenging, singing through on counts can help emphasize the rhythmic relationships. Count singing is shown in example 5.10.

CONCLUSION

Sight-singing in the choral rehearsal is not an all-or-nothing proposition but a matter of degrees. Envisioning the choir program in levels can help to create a year-to-year sequence for skill development without losing the students' interest. Choosing some simpler literature for its reading potential can build students' confidence in their ability and allow directors to focus on musical concerns that are sometimes less evident in more difficult selections. Finally, the director committed to sight-singing has a responsibility to integrate reading challenges within the teaching of a new

EXAMPLE 5.10. COUNT SINGING IN THE SOPRANO AND ALTO PARTS OF VECCHI'S "IO SOFFRIRO."

piece. This approach not only develops a feeling of success but also helps draw attention to the structural qualities of the literature. Understanding music structurally leads to more intelligent musicianship and more musical performances.

RECOMMENDED READINGS

Bertalot, John (1993). *Five wheels to successful sight-singing.* Minneapolis: Augsburg Fortress.

McCoy, C. W. (1989). Basic training: Working with inexperienced choirs. *Music Educators Journal, 75* (8), 42–45.

Phillips, K. H. (1996). Teaching singers to sight-read. *Teaching Music, 3* (6), 32–33.

6

Sight-Singing Assessment Procedures

Q. How many student in a class of thirty-five need to be able to
sight-sing a tonal pattern in order for the teacher to hear "the
class" sight-singing?

A. Often, only one.

Peggy Bennett

In an article titled, "Tricks, Masks, and Camouflage: Is Imitation Passing for Music Reading?" Peggy Bennett discusses the problem of choir members with weaker musical skills getting in the habit of following or imitating leaders in their section. Choir directors know that it only takes a few good readers spread among the sections to improve the entire choir's ability to sight-read and learn new music. While this is a benefit to group progress, it hides many problems with individual skill development. Research on individual sight-singing performance in choirs with good group sight-singing ability confirms Bennett's suspicions, revealing a wide range of individual reading skills (Demorest & May, 1995; Henry & Demorest, 1994).

This deception on the part of the students is not purposeful. It is a survival skill that students develop quite unconsciously—the ability to follow either a singing leader or keyboard doubling by being just a split second behind the note. Often students may believe that they are good readers when, in fact, they have simply become expert followers. One of my students encountered individual sight-singing tests for the first time in his college music education course. Up until that point, new music had been either read as a class in his aural skills courses or prepared ahead of time for "reading" tests at the end of the term. As he put it, "I really thought I was a pretty good reader until I had to sing a piece I had never seen before by myself." That is why evaluation is such an important component of any sight-singing curriculum. It is the only reliable means of assessing a student's individual development and identifying areas for further work. Without it, both the student and the teacher may believe that everything is fine when, in fact, it is not.

Given the importance of assessment in evaluating the success of instruction, one would expect it to figure prominently in many published sight-singing materials, yet it does not. Only since the publication of the *National Standards* in 1994 have music teachers begun to look seriously at individual assessment. Surveys of choral directors prior to that time indicate that as few as 1 in 10 do any kind of regular formal evaluation of their students' sight-singing ability. This is not too surprising considering the limited assessment training music teachers often receive. As S. C. Shuler suggests, "Music educators need practical training in assessment as a natural and necessary part of the teaching/learning process" (1996, p. 89). This chapter will present several models for different kinds of assessment that can help determine how well students are learning to sight-sing and how to develop their skills further. Assessment procedures for both groups and individuals are presented first, followed by scoring procedures and grading.

GROUP SIGHT-SINGING ASSESSMENT

Group assessment is the form of evaluation that is probably most familiar to choir directors, since ensemble sight-reading is becoming more common at various contests and festivals. While individual progress is the primary goal of any instruction, there are skills associated with group sight-singing that will have a direct benefit in rehearsal. It is also important that students become comfortable reading in a multipart context. When reading as a group, students should be looking and listening carefully and developing self-evaluation skills. Since a piece is only *sight*-read once, students should be able to:

1. Scan the music and identify potential problem spots.
2. Audiate pitch and rhythm patterns prior to reading.
3. Detect and correct errors from one reading to the next.

Several well-established procedures for group reading are available; the most common are those used for large-group contest sight-singing. An example of such procedures, taken from the Texas University Interscholastic League Music Contest, is shown in figure 6.1. Notice how similar this sequence is to the multipart sight-singing procedures presented in chapter 4. Students are required to study the music and assess errors with

FIGURE 6.1. TEXAS UIL MUSIC CONTEST SIGHT-SINGING PROCEDURES.

Texas UIL Procedures for Choral Sight-Reading Competition.

1. Time. A director of a choral group will be given six minutes to study the score and instruct the organization.
2. Instructions. At any time during the instruction period the tonic chord may be played once in broken chord style. It may not be reproduced by the students. The director may instruct the group by tapping out rhythms and talking about any passage of music but may not hum, sing any part, or allow it to be played on the piano. Students may chant rhythms or text and tap or clap the rhythms. But they may not reproduce the music tonally. Students may ask questions and make comments, according to the director's wishes.
3. Marking Music. Neither the director nor the students may mark on the sightreading music unless instructed to do so by a judge.
4. First Reading. At the completion of the instruction period, choral groups will be given the tonic chord, in broken chord style. At that time, the students may reproduce the tonic chord, utilizing their preferred method of sightreading (numbers, syllables, etc.). The accompanist will then give the starting pitches, which each section may sing, again utilizing their preferred method. The director may sing the starting pitch with each section. No further warm-up or instruction by the director is permitted, including the use of verbal counting to initiate the reading. The selection will then be sung without piano accompaniment and using the group's preferred method of sightreading. The director may choose to read the piece in the printed key or any other key suitable for the group.
5. Second Instruction Period. Following the first reading, the director will have two minutes for instruction. The procedures described in (2) will apply.
6. Second Reading. The procedures in (4) will apply. The selection will then be sung a cappella. All groups may continue to use their preferred method of sightreading or may sing the words printed in the score. The director's decision to use text or not will have no bearing on the final rating. Both readings will be judged.
7. Disqualification. A choral group whose director makes an obvious contribution to the performance by either singing with or speaking to the students or making other audible contributions while they are performing will be disqualified. An obvious attempt by a director to be disqualified may result in a rating. (A judge's decision of what is obvious is final.)

---

limited help from the teacher. To make this procedure more challenging, step 2 could be altered to study time for the students without aid of the instructor. The teacher could then either insert questions about the music before reading or just proceed directly to reading. The Texas procedures feature the chance to read the piece twice; this is important for evaluating the group's ability to detect and correct errors from one reading to the next.

Group reading also can be the starting point for individual assessment. Preparatory questions can be asked of individuals at random in such a way that different students are responsible for providing information about meter, key, starting syllable, and so on, and all students know that they may be responsible for providing the information. While this does not directly assess students' reading ability, it does let the teacher know if they can identify the musical characteristics necessary to read successfully. Having individuals read or recognize short pitch and rhythm patterns on the board also can be incorporated into this questioning procedure. Questions are asked of individuals either at random or by calling on every third or fourth student in the row. Answering questions should be seen as the responsibility of everyone in the group, not as a punishment for not paying attention. One example is given in figure 6.2.

FIGURE 6–2. INDIVIDUAL ASSESSMENT DURING GROUP READING.

German Folk Melody from the Oxford *Folk Song Sight-singing Series* Vol. 1, #20.

Teacher	"Joe, what is the time signature for this piece?"
Joe	3/4
Teacher	"Robin, what does 3/4 mean?"
Robin	"There are three beats in a measure and the quarter note gets the beat."
Teacher	"Ryan, what is the key signature?"
Ryan	"One flat."
Teacher	"And what key does that represent?"
Ryan	"F major."
Teacher	"Jessica, how do we know it's F major?"
Jessica	"It begins and ends on F and if you count down four lines and spaces from the flat it falls on f."
Teacher	"Claire, what is 'do' in F major?"
Claire	"f."
Teacher	"Are there any repeating patterns?"
Robert	"Yes. Both four-measure phrases are repeated."

→

FIGURE 6.2. continued

Teacher   "Robert, would you chant the rhythm of the first four measures on tas and tis?"
Robert chants the rhythm.
Teacher   "You have 30 seconds to scan and then we'll sing it. Don't forget about dynamics."
Students scan and then sing.

DIAGNOSTIC ASSESSMENT

Diagnostic assessment is often the only type of individual assessment done in choral ensembles, and it is usually done during auditions to determine membership. Many conductors include sight-singing and tonal memory tests in auditions in order to assess students' ability prior to admitting them into an ensemble. Unfortunately, the results often are used only to determine group membership when, in fact, they can be a valuable resource for determining where instruction should begin.

Unlike auditions, where the stakes are high and nerves are often frayed, diagnostic assessment of students' sight-singing ability should be as non-threatening as possible. The goal is to find out what they know, not what they do not. A common complaint of secondary teachers is, "The elementary teacher did not teach them anything about sight-singing before they got here." It simply may be that the previous teacher used different terminology or a different approach and the secondary choir director has never taken the time to coordinate their program with earlier instruction. The students often suffer because they are confronted with an entirely new system and little help in connecting it to their previous learning.

The first step in diagnostic assessment is to find out how (or if) sight-singing was taught at the elementary (or middle school) level. This will allow you to tie into the students' previous learning and accurately assess what they know before they begin your program. Obviously this will not help assess the ability of students who are new to the district. For these students, some open-ended questions about how they would approach learning a new piece or a multiple choice of different syllable systems may help to address their skill level. After having determined what students should be able to do, design a simple test to identify how well individuals have learned to read.

A sample of some possible items for a diagnostic assessment is given in figure 6.3. The items focus on students' aural skills and analytical ability rather than their written knowledge of musical symbols and terms. A

FIGURE 6.3. SAMPLE ITEMS FROM DIAGNOSTIC ASSESSMENT.

See and Hear

I. Identifying Rhythm Patterns
Directions: You will hear one measure of steady beat to set the tempo and then each example will be played three times. Compare what you hear to each of the three examples (A B C) given for each item.

II. Identifying Pitch Patterns
Directions: All of these examples are in the same key. You will hear the scale each time (do to do) followed by the pattern. Each example will be played three times. Compare what you hear to each of the three examples (A B C) given for each item.

3. A. d–m–s–m–d   B. d–r–m–r–d   C. d–s–l–s–d

4. A. d–t₁–l₁–s₁–d   B. d–s₁–f₁–s₁–d   C. d–s₁–l₁–s₁–d

III. Error Detection
Directions: For the following example, identify the key signature, time signature, and starting syllable. The pattern will be sung three times on solfège. Compare the sung pattern to the music notated on your paper and circle any wrong pitches or rhythms.

_____ Key Signature
_____ Time Signature
_____ Starting Syllable

IV. Performance
Directions: Go into the practice room, turn on the tape recorder, and speak your name slowly and clearly. Then sing a major scale (do to do) on solfège in any key. In the same key, sing this pattern:
d–m–s–m–d–f–l–f–t₁–r–s–t₁–d.

written component can be helpful, but it will not reveal anything about students' music-reading ability. The diagnostic assessment should be given sometime in the first few weeks, though probably not the first day. In addition to this group-administered assessment, an individual sight-singing assessment would be very informative. This can be done several ways.

Individual Meetings

Some directors like to hear all of their students individually or in small groups at the beginning of the year to assess vocal status and/or problems. It would be simple to slip in some music reading. See if the students can sing simple pitch patterns from solfège or speak a simple rhythm. Failing that, have them try echoing pitch and rhythm patterns you give them to check ear and memory skills and to introduce the syllables.

Taped Tests

In addition to the taped performance portion of the diagnostic assessment, students could sight-sing on tape. One way to accomplish this is to have students read several simple melodies as a group on pitch and rhythm syllables the first week and then choose one of those melodies as an individual sight-singing melody. Though the students are not really *sight*-reading, the teacher gets a sense of their ability to hold a key and reproduce a melodic pattern on syllables. While singing into a tape recorder may seem daunting at first, this procedure is often less threatening than singing in front of the director or peers. It also introduces students to an assessment procedure that you can use throughout the year. Two procedures for taped sight-singing assessments are given in figures 6.4 and 6.5.

FIGURE 6.4. STEPS IN THE EVALUATIVE ASSESSMENT PROCEDURE.

1. The student enters a room with two tape recorders. Tape 1 contains directions; Tape 2 is for recording their sight-singing.
2. The student hits "Play" on tape recorder 1, the instruction tape.
3. The student is asked to open the folder with the test example; the tape then plays the tonic chord and a starting pitch and instructs the student to study the example for 30 seconds.
4. The student is then told to press "Record" on tape recorder 2 and say their name. The key and starting pitch are given again on tape 1, followed by another 30 seconds of silence for the student to sing the melody.
5. The instruction tape then tells the student to turn off tape recorder 2 and rewind the instruction tape for the next student.

FIGURE 6.5. STEPS IN THE PRACTICE ASSESSMENT PROCEDURE.

1. In the hallway outside the testing room, there is a music stand with a folder. The student opens the folder and looks at the sight-singing example.
2. When the previous student is finished, the student enters the practice room and opens the folder in the practice room that contains the same example.
3. The student hits the "Record" button on the tape recorder and gives their name.
4. The student then sings the tonic triad or some other solfège or number pattern to establish the key; they tap two measures in the tempo they wish to sing and begin singing the melody.
5. When they are finished, they hit the "Stop" button and leave.

INDIVIDUAL ASSESSMENT

As mentioned at the beginning of the chapter, it is possible for an ensemble to read well even though many students have not developed individual sight-singing skills. That is why individual assessment is crucial. Teachers are accountable for the individual achievement of students in addition to the achievement of the ensemble. However, individual assessment is a time-consuming process. Unlike regular classroom instructors, who teach 25 to 30 students in each class, choral teachers can be faced with 60 to 100 students in a single ensemble. The prospect of tracking each student's progress can seem so overwhelming that many teachers never begin, despite the potential benefits to their students and their program.

Fortunately, individual assessment seems to have benefits beyond simply informing the teacher of student progress and can be accomplished with minimal disruption to rehearsal. Research I have conducted (1998a) has looked at the potential benefits of a systematic program of individual assessment combined with regular group reading instruction and found that students who received individual assessment opportunities improved significantly more than those who received only group instruction. It is likely that individual testing helps students to transfer the skills they are learning in the group to individual reading challenges by motivating students to practice their skills and by identifying specific areas for personal improvement.

What teachers need are time-efficient strategies for implementing individual assessment, making it a feasible addition to the choral program. The goal is to create minimal disruption of regular rehearsal procedures and also minimize the time needed to evaluate student work. The remainder of this chapter is devoted to presenting efficient and effective strategies for recording, scoring, and giving feedback for individual sight-singing assessment.

Taped Assessment

Taping provides a time-efficient way to administer sight-singing exams, though the scoring is still time-consuming. The taping procedure can take two forms. The first, *evaluative*, form of the taped test is summarized in figure 6.4. This procedure can be used throughout the year to document student progress.

The second approach to taped testing has a more pedagogical focus; this *practice* test requires only one tape recorder, because the students are going to set their own tempo and key for singing. One week prior to their practice test the students are each given a sheet of single-line melodies. They are shown how to practice on their own and perhaps even given a handout that outlines practice procedures. The students are told that one of these melodies will be chosen for their sight-singing test the following week. The procedure, given in figure 6.5, is done during rehearsal the following week. If there are four rooms, there can be one taping room for each section. No more than two students per section are gone at any one time, and the returning person alerts the next one to go out to the room so that the teacher need not stop and start rehearsal. Ideally either the testing rooms have no piano or the piano is turned so that the keyboard faces the wall. Plan on spending some time in logistics when this procedure is introduced, but if it is used regularly the students will quickly understand the routine. Once the students are used to the procedure, testing can be accomplished in a day and with little interruption in rehearsal.

The procedures given here are identical to those used in my research study on individual testing (Demorest, 1998a). The students in the experimental groups were given the *practice* test once a month, or three times a semester. No effort was made to track the amount of practicing that they did in the week prior to testing. Still the experimental choirs outperformed the control groups on the *evaluative* test, which involved sight-singing a melody they had never seen.

Quartet Testing

Some teachers prefer testing in quartets to provide a more "authentic" assessment of students' choral sight-singing abilities. While each student is responsible for their part individually, they still have to read in a four-part context and function as a member of a group. In addition, the singers get the benefit of a harmonic context to help them find their part. The only problem with this kind of assessment is the interdependency of the quartet members. It is harder to sight-sing a line with the wrong notes being sung next to you than it is to do it by yourself. One possible alternative is the "virtual" quartet. By using a computer with MIDI sequencing capabilities the teacher can record all four parts of a choral example with a starting chord and a click track for tempo. The student can then go into the room alone and turn off *their* part of the piece, turn on the tape recorder and say their name, and start the sequence. The computer will fill in the other three voices accurately while the student supplies the fourth. This has the added advantage of forcing the student to keep going, since the program will not stop for them. Figure 6.6 shows a computer screen from *Performer* with the tenor part muted for testing.

Computer Testing

The use of a MIDI virtual quartet is similar to another possible option for assessment. Computer technology is rapidly moving from the strict drill and practice model of electronic "flash cards" to a more sophisticated form of practicing that can actually record and evaluate students' attempts at music reading. There is only one program on the market to date that can record a student's sight-singing attempt and score it based on percentages of correct pitch and rhythm. Musicware's *Music Lab Melody*, version 3.0d (1997), offers students drill and practice opportunities on a variety of content areas, including note names, interval identification,

FIGURE 6.6. SCREEN FOR TENOR QUARTET ASSESSMENT USING *PERFORMER*. VERSION 6.01. (MOTU, 1997.)

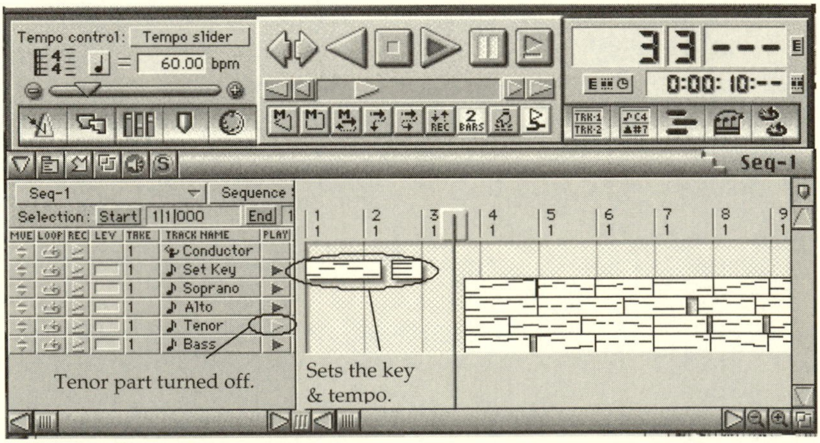

echoing and reading rhythm patterns, and other more traditional computerized music-practice activities. One module presents students with melodies to sight-sing at many different levels of difficulty. The melodies are sequenced for difficulty within each level, but students can choose to start at different levels for practice. However, the assessment portion called "quizzes" has to begin with level 1.

The advantages of a computerized approach are in the areas of record keeping and scoring. The program keeps track of student progress, but also records the amount of time students spend practicing. *Music Lab Melody,* version 3.0d, scores students' performance as a percentage of correct pitches and rhythms. However, there are still some problems with the computer's definition of *correct*. Correct rhythm depends on students' absolute accuracy when compared to a click track. While it can be quantized to be sensitive to different note values, anyone who has ever tried to accurately sequence a song using a click track knows how difficult that kind of accuracy is. The pitch evaluation does not respond well to low voices, richer vocal timbres, stronger singing, or broader vowels. The computer is happiest when one sings with a very unattractive straight, nasal tone and uses a very mechanical rhythmic approach. Despite some drawbacks in current technology that will no doubt be corrected eventually, the program offers many worthwhile features. It gives students real-time visual feedback on their pitch accuracy, which can be used both for sight-singing and for pitch-matching and intonation problems.

SCORING SYSTEMS

The method a teacher chooses to score sight-singing is independent of the assessment procedures used. Regardless of live or taped assessment, group or individual assessment, any scoring system can be employed. The choice of a scoring system is based on the kind of information you want to communicate to students and how you wish their progress to be reported. There are three basic types: criterion scoring, numerical scoring, and rubrics.

Criterion Scoring

This is the simplest of the scoring procedures because it is essentially pass/fail. The difficulty of the melody represents a particular level of achievement. Once a student can accurately read melodies at a particular difficulty level, they have met the criteria and may move on. This type of scoring is common if sight-singing is only one component of student progress that is being assessed.

FIGURE 6.7. ADDITIVE CRITERION SCORING FORM FOR SIGHT-SINGING.

Sight-Singing Level 2
1. Retained the original key throughout the example   _____
2. Kept a steady tempo throughout the example   _____
3. Majority of pitches were accurate and in tune   _____
4. Majority of rhythms were accurate   _____
5. Expressive markings were realized in performance   _____
                                    TOTAL SCORE   _____

Comments:

If teachers want to give the students more information than pass or fail, they can break sight-singing down into component criteria and use an "additive" scoring system. In additive scoring, the sight-singing task at any level is broken down into components such as "retained key," "kept steady tempo," "accurate pitches," "accurate rhythm," and "expressive markings followed." The student's score is simply the sum of all items checked. This has the advantage of letting students know more specifically where they have succeeded and where they still need work. An example of additive criterion scoring is given in figure 6.7. The highest possible score is 5, with 1 point for each item. The teacher can set a score such as 4 or 4.5 as the passing mark to move on to the next level.

Numerical Scoring

Numerical scoring can take two forms, as either a point system based on the number of correct notes or measures or a rating scale that reflects extent of achievement. Point systems are designed to award points for correct elements such as correct pitches or correct rhythms. Point scoring is very objective and reliable because it treats each element, whether a note or a measure, as a point and simply records whether or not that element was accurate. It also can translate easily into a grade. Figure 6.8 is an example of a 15-note sight-singing excerpt that has been scored using a point system.

The numerical system awards 1 point per note, ½ for correct pitch and ½ for correct rhythm. Thus the 15-note melody in figure 6.8 would be worth 15 points, 7.5 for pitch and 7.5 for rhythm. Pitch errors can be circled and rhythm errors marked with an "x" while listening to the example. It usually takes at least two hearings to catch everything. Teachers can subtract points for inconsistent tempo or for starting over, because those difficulties could affect the overall performance score. This

FIGURE 6.8. EXAMPLE OF A POINT SYSTEM FOR SCORING SIGHT-SINGING.

Rhythm __4.5__   Pitch __5.5__   Tempo __OK__   Restart __OK__   TOTAL __10__ (15)

type of scoring is more difficult to use, but it does separate pitch and rhythm difficulties, which allows the teacher to see where work needs to be done. A simpler version of numerical scoring awards 1 point per measure of the example. Thus an eight-measure melody is worth 8 points. The teacher can still record the kinds of errors heard in written comments for the student and can give partial credit for a measure with only one error.

Rating scales are a variation on the additive scoring system. Instead of awarding 1 point per item, the teacher evaluates each item on a scale that reflects the level of performance. Figure 6.9 illustrates an application of the rating scale to the additive scoring form.

Rubrics

Perhaps the most useful scoring system is the rubric. It combines a numerical score with comments as to what was successful and what needs work. This is the type of scoring that is often used to assess such subjective and complicated skills as writing ability and composition, but it is equally informative for skills such as music reading. In a rubric, each point is tied to a description of the level of competence. Ideally, these compe-

FIGURE 6.9. A RATING SCALE SCORING SYSTEM.

Sight-Singing Level 2					
	Needs Improvement			Outstanding	
1. Retained the original key throughout the example	1	2	3	4	5
2. Kept a steady tempo throughout the example	1	2	3	4	5
3. Majority of pitches were accurate and in tune	1	2	3	4	5
4. Majority of rhythms were accurate	1	2	3	4	5
5. Expressive markings were realized in performance	1	2	3	4	5
TOTAL SCORE				_____	
Comments:					

tencies are stated in terms of what the student can do, not what they cannot do. An example of a sight-singing rubric is given in figure 6.10.

FEEDBACK

A good scoring system provides a consistent and meaningful way to record and report student progress, but it does not necessarily give students all the information they need in order to improve their skill. As mentioned

FIGURE 6.10. SIGHT-SINGING SCORING RUBRIC.

Individual Sight-Singing Evaluation

Pitch

5	Pitches were accurate throughout.
4	Strong tonal center, most pitches correct, a few intervals were incorrect.
3	Good sense of key, awareness of tonic throughout.
2	Correct starting pitch, key center changed throughout.
1	Missed starting pitch, no clear sense of key.

Rhythm

5	Steady tempo and accurate rhythms throughout.
4	Steady tempo, missed a few rhythmic patterns in the line.
3	Kept sense of steady beat but with fluctuating tempo, several rhythmic patterns incorrect.
2	Started in a tempo, but lost sense of steady beat. Stopping or slowing on certain patterns.
1	Inconsistent beat from the beginning. Stopping and/or starting over repeatedly.

Expression

5	Sung expressively with good tone, clear phrasing and accurate dynamic level and dynamic shading.
4	Sung expressively with accurate phrasing and general dynamic level. Lack of dynamic shading and nuance.
3	Sung with good tone and accurate phrasing. Did not reflect accurate dynamic level or dynamic changes.
2	Sung with good tone, but with little attention to phrasing or dynamics.
1	Sung with inconsistent tone and no clear sense of phrasing or general dynamic level.

____ Total Score

Comments:

---

before, rubrics offer an opportunity for students to receive a score with a description of what was achieved and what needs improvement. These descriptions are, by necessity, brief and somewhat general. They are not usually sufficient feedback for guiding a student's further study. Feedback from the teacher on areas for individual work is crucial to fostering individual progress. Feedback can take a number of forms, such as written comments, checklists, taped comments, and computerized responses.

Written Comments

If a teacher chooses to use one of the numerical scoring systems, then the score needs to be supplemented by written comments that explain the strengths and weaknesses of the performance. Written feedback is the teacher's opportunity to individualize instruction by identifying areas where each individual student needs improvement. Recognizing individual student achievement as well as future needs adds an important dimension to choral music education and helps the teacher to identify some of the larger problems regarding students' skills. Written feedback is also extremely time-consuming, as any English teacher will tell you.

Checklists

Teachers who provide written feedback often find themselves saying many of the same things over and over (many of us have experienced this phenomenon while judging choral and solo contests—"deeper breath," "more supported sound," "dropped jaw," etc.). As one develops a sense of where the common problems are, a checklist can be developed that describes many of the common problems and recommended solutions. The checklist has the advantage of being less time-consuming while still allowing the teacher to give specific individual feedback. If a problem is encountered that is not on the list, there is still the opportunity to write a comment. An example of a sight-singing feedback checklist is given in figure 6.11.

Many of the comments in the checklist are similar to those in the rubric but more detailed and connected to suggestions on how to improve. One of the other uses of a checklist is to let students know in advance where the problems and pitfalls of sight-singing may be. If they are given a comment checklist prior to testing, they have a sense of what the teacher is listening for in the assessment, as well as suggestions on how to practice.

Taped Comments

Some teachers utilize audiotape not only for assessment but also for feedback. Students turn in their taped assessment by a particular date, usu-

FIGURE 6.11. SIGHT-SINGING FEEDBACK CHECKLIST.

Sight-Singing Assessment

Name _____   Level _____   Score _____

Practice for next time:

Key Accuracy

_____ need to be sure to identify do/la correctly

_____ need to establish the tonic and dominant

_____ need to keep scale in mind as you sing

_____ need to keep I/IV/V triads in mind

Pitch Accuracy

_____ changed key during example

_____ pitches correct but sharp/flat

_____ some intervals were consistently a problem:

    m2   M2   m3
    M3   P4   tt
    P5   m6   M6
    m7   M7   P8

_____ sang right pitches but wrong syllables

_____ sang right syllables but wrong pitches

Tempo

_____ need to clearly establish the steady beat before starting

_____ tendency to rush/drag

_____ tendency to pause or restart

Rhythmic Accuracy

_____ need to keep the beat clearly

_____ some notes values consistently too long/short: 1/16 1/8 1/4 1/2 1/1

Other

_____ keep counting through longer note values

_____ practice counting: (fill in rhythm)

_____ check values of rests

Expressive

_____ need open, accurate vowels on solfege

_____ need a deep, supporting breath to sing

_____ need to reflect dynamic markings in your singing

_____ sing with dynamic variation in line

_____ breathe at phrase breaks, not between

Other Comments:

Pitch/Key Accuracy

_____ review finding do/la from key signature

_____ sing d m s m d f l f t, r s t, d in the key before reading melody

_____ sing full scale in solfege before reading melody

_____ check "do" as you are practicing reading

_____ scan melodies for difficult intervals and sing before reading

_____ sing chord outlines while playing chord on piano

_____ sing familiar melodies in solfège

Rhythm/Tempo Accuracy

_____ tap two measures in tempo before beginning sight-singing

_____ chant the rhythm on counts/ syllables while keeping a steady beat

_____ chant the rhythm on solfege while keeping a steady beat

_____ sight-sing with the metronome, and tap the beat

_____ practice setting the beat in different tempos, with and without metronome

_____ scan for difficult patterns and chant through rhythms before reading

Expressive

_____ sing different warmups on solfege syllables, concentrating on vocal tone

_____ sing up the scale on solfege, concentrating on good tone and support

_____ scan for dynamic markings before singing

_____ scan for phrase markings before singing

_____ practice sight-singing at different dynamic levels

_____ sight-sing a new melody once through and then sing one phrase at a time

ally by depositing the completed tape in an envelope or box in the teacher's office. The teacher then listens to the tapes on a portable cassette recorder and records their feedback immediately following the assessment example. Students can listen to the tape and hear the teacher's comments. Taped feedback is most efficient if the teacher is using criterion scoring, where the judgment is simply pass or fail at a particular level. If numerical scoring is used, then there is usually a written component, and taping comments does not necessarily save time. Many students value the detail and personalized nature of taped comments, not unlike the procedures favored by many judges at large group festivals.

Computerized Responses

Computer programs designed for practicing ear-training skills or even evaluating sight-singing are designed to give immediate feedback on students' performance, but the nature of this feedback varies. The most simplistic programs record a right or wrong score for each example and perhaps provide encouraging statements along the way such as, "Good work!" or "Not quite—try again." More advanced programs can give students information on the nature of the problem through either written responses such as "too low" or visual feedback. For example, some interval identification programs will display the interval that the student chose in comparison to the interval that was played; some even play the incorrect choice so that the student can hear the difference. *Music Lab Melody*, version 3.0d, a sight-singing program, provides real-time visual feedback of where the student is singing versus the notated example, so that the student can attempt to correct themselves while singing. An example of the visual feedback is given in figure 6.12. Example A shows the program in its "tuning" mode, where the student can establish their accuracy on the different solfège syllables prior to sight-singing. The target pitch is highlighted while the diamonds indicate in real time how high or low the singer is in relation to the pitch. Example B shows the feedback given after a student has sight-read the melody. The graphic display shows where the voice (wavy line) was relative to the target pitches (icon bars) for that example.

GRADING

While assessment offers the teacher a means of tracking and recording student learning over a period of time, it is not the same thing as grading. Grading involves assigning a certain value to the different activities students engage in and then assigning a letter or number to the students'

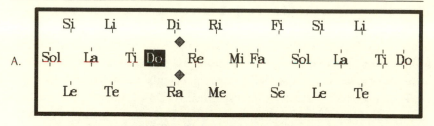

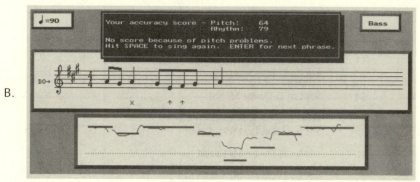

performance in that area according to some standard. While assessment and grading are different activities, ideally they are interrelated. Sight-singing has typically not been a large part of choral teachers' grading, in part because of a lack of individual assessment. Another challenge is the wide range of musical abilities found in most choral programs. However, once a student's ability level has been identified through diagnostic assessment, grades can be based on progress from point A to point B, as measured by regular assessment. This is most easily done when skills are organized according to different levels so that both the students and teachers are more aware of the progress. Skill-level assessments can be tied to the *National Standards* or to a published choral series text such as *Essential Musicianship* or *Choral Connections*. If a teacher values the skill of sight-singing, then progress in that area should be reflected in the student's grade.

SUMMARY

There is no question that assessment has become a more critical topic in music education over the last 5 to 10 years. Teachers are looking for efficient and effective strategies for evaluating student progress in a number of areas. Individual assessment of sight-singing is crucial for two reasons: 1) research has shown that group sight-singing achievement is not a valid indicator of individual skills; and 2) research also indicates that regular assessment actually improves student learning in the area of sight-singing. The key is to find an assessment procedure that makes sense and use it consistently.

Evaluating individual progress takes more time than not doing it, but there is also no question that teachers must attend to individual skill development if they wish to provide evidence of student learning. The benefits to the ensemble of having more skilled members are obvious, and thus individual skill development can actually save time in the long term, as literature can be learned more rapidly and musically. Over the years, I have noticed that there are two kinds of singers: those who consider themselves "readers" and those who do not. What is interesting about that perception is that the difference in ability level between those two groups is not always that great. The statement is more reflective of a singer's attitude toward reading. The sense of accomplishment that students experience as they progress through a sight-singing curriculum can give them the confidence they need to begin to think of themselves as readers.

RECOMMENDED READINGS

Brinson, B. A. (1996). *Choral music methods and materials: Developing successful choral programs.* (Chapter 4.) New York: Schirmer.

Demorest, S. M. (1998). Improving sight-singing performance in the choral ensemble: The effect of individual testing. *Journal of Research in Music Education, 46,* 182–192.

Keenan-Takagi, K. (2000). Embedded assessment in the middle school choral ensemble. *Music Educators Journal,* 86(4), 42–46, 63.

Shuler, S. C. (1996). The effects of the National Standards on assessment (and vice versa). In *Aiming for excellence: The impact of the standards movement on music education.* Reston, VA: Music Educators National Conference.

PART III

What Materials Are Available?

A s mentioned in chapter 4, a teacher must determine what skills to teach the students and in what sequence. If a teacher does not have a lot of personal experience with sight-singing instruction, deciding where to begin and what material to use can be a daunting task. Fortunately, there are some very fine publications that can help beginning teachers in a number of ways. Many of these books provide sight-singing exercises that are sequenced by difficulty and organized into units of study. In addition, some books provide teaching suggestions, visual aids, and even literature that corresponds to what the students are learning. While no book will meet all the specific needs of each teacher's unique situation, a good sight-singing series can provide a framework for organizing a comprehensive skills curriculum.

The final two chapters review published sight-singing materials available for secondary choral teachers. Chapter 7 discusses the results of a Web survey that asked practicing teachers what kinds of sight-singing materials they used and why. Chapter 8 provides a review of 21 sets of published sight-singing materials. Summaries regarding organization and content are designed to help teachers identify materials that they think would best fit their needs. Many of these collections feature carefully sequenced materials and clearly written goals and objectives for each level of achievement. They can be a great help to teachers in determining their students' sight-singing curriculum.

7

Materials

There is no good musician who does not hear what he sees and does not see what he hears.

Zoltán Kodály

One of the most common problems for beginning teachers interested in teaching sight-singing is locating materials that fit the skill levels and needs of their various choirs. This chapter reports survey results regarding the kinds of sight-singing materials choir teachers are using currently and what they feel are the most important features to look for in choosing materials. Chapter 8 then provides an annotated listing of currently available sight-singing materials. The goal of these chapters is not to provide a single recommended list of materials, because each teaching situation has different priorities and different needs; one teacher may want a set of graded materials, a second prefers a method-specific approach, while a third wants a good collection of existing melodies to sing. The goal is to provide information that will allow teachers to make informed choices about the materials they use in instruction.

SIGHT-SINGING MATERIALS SURVEY RESULTS

Several of the surveys mentioned in chapter 2 report that choral directors often prefer to use octavos or self-created materials to teach sight-singing (Hales, 1961; Johnson, 1987; May, 1993). While some teachers reported using commercially published sight-singing materials, they were in the minority. Perhaps this was due in part to the expense of purchasing published materials or to a lack of information about available choices. The Web survey of choral directors discussed in chapters 2 and 3 included questions about what materials teachers use and how often they use them. Figure 7.1 lists the top 12 sight-singing materials used by the 178 choral directors who responded to the survey. All other available materials were mentioned by fewer than 10% of the directors who responded. The teachers were asked to indicate the frequency of use based on a five-point scale that ranged from 1 (Never) to 5 (Always). The mean frequency of use indicates not only how many directors used the material but also how often. The higher the number, the more frequent the use.

As with earlier surveys, four of the five most used sight-singing materials were either created by the directors or taken from music not specifically intended for sight-singing instruction. The large percentage of directors who use self-created materials is not surprising. They report needing exercises that fit specific problems they would encounter in the literature. Many teachers report creating examples based on music from the pieces being rehearsed. Music notation programs appear to be very popular with directors, and many report using Finale or Encore to create examples for their students. One director reports having the advanced choir students create a book of original sight-singing melodies for the other choirs based on the melodies in the Oxford *Folk Song Sight-Singing Series*.

The use of octavos may reflect teachers who integrate sight-singing into rehearsal of the literature or teachers who have a collection of pieces they use only for reading practice. Hymnals have always been popular for multipart sight-singing practice, in part because of their low cost. If you can find a church that is switching to a new hymnal, the old ones are often donated or available at a fraction of the cost. For relatively little expense, a director can have hundreds of singable and relatively easy four-

FIGURE 7.1. THE MOST COMMONLY USED SIGHT-SINGING MATERIALS REPORTED IN THE SURVEY.

Title	%	Mean frequency of use
Self-created materials	77	2.94
Octavos	48	2.16
Hymnals	32	1.78
Jenson Sight-singing Course	27	1.72
Bach Chorales	25	1.51
Successful Sight-singing	22	1.49
Essential Musicianship	21	1.53
Choral Approach to Sight-singing	19	1.39
Patterns of Sound	16	1.34
The Sight-singer	13	1.29
Melodia	11	1.25
Kodàly Choral Method	11	1.21

part songs. One note of caution: Many directors who use hymnals for sight-reading have found it necessary to go through the painstaking process of whiting out all of the text to avoid problems with promoting religion in their curriculum.

While 4 of the top 5 choices in the materials survey are not sight-singing publications, commercial publications are well represented in the top 12, including two relative newcomers, *Essential Musicianship* (1995) and *Successful Sight-Singing* (1992). Their inclusion may reflect choir teachers' growing interest in a more structured, comprehensive approach to teaching sight-singing. This interest might be based in part on the *National Standards* movement and its increased focus on assessment. It also may reflect a general improvement in the quality of the materials themselves. Both of the books mentioned, while different in content, present a very "musical" approach to teaching music reading that emphasizes a connection to choral literature.

IMPORTANT FEATURES OF SIGHT-SINGING MATERIALS

The Web survey also asked teachers to rate the importance of various features in their selection of teaching materials. These questions were included to provide insight on what qualities are most valued in published sight-singing texts. The ratings also provided a basis for creating a review form that identifies and summarizes the different features of published sight-singing materials. Teachers were asked to rate the importance on a scale from 1 (Not Important) to 5 (Very Important). The features are listed in order of importance in figure 7.2.

Teachers also were asked to mention any attributes they felt were important but that were not included on the list. The most frequently mentioned consideration was that the material *not* be method-specific. Flexibility was considered an important feature. Other frequently men-

FIGURE 7.2. FEATURES OF SIGHT-SINGING MATERIALS.

1. The material is graded for difficulty.
2. The material includes minor melodies.
3. The material features separate pitch- and rhythm-reading activities.
4. The material provides evaluation opportunities.
5. The material includes music theory information.
6. The material is method-specific (e.g., includes a method for teaching and model lessons).
7. The material is drawn from existing music.
8. The material includes modal melodies.

tioned concerns were that: 1) the material be sequential, with lots of repetition at a particular level before increasing difficulty; 2) it include treble and bass clefs and multiple voicings; 3) the ranges be smaller for junior high boys; 4) materials be easy to read and to handle (size); and 5) some melodies contain text or correlated literature be provided. Flexibility seems to be the most valued attribute. Teachers want materials that can be used at many skill levels and with many voicings, that do not require a particular teaching approach, and that prepare students for real music (though they need not be drawn from "real" music themselves).

REVIEWING CHORAL SIGHT-SINGING MATERIALS

The teachers' ratings of various attributes were used to help create a form for reviewing the content of published sight-singing materials (fig. 7.3). For each publication, the summary begins with basic bibliographic and purchasing information. Organization and content are discussed in terms of level, sequence, musical material, method, and evaluation. The organization and content section covers the scope of the series. That is, if there are three volumes that represent three different levels, the summary refers to the scope of all three volumes combined. The strengths and weaknesses of each publication appear in the section titled "Distinguishing Features."

This form was used to review 21 of the published materials currently available for sight-singing instruction. While the list itself will become dated rather quickly, the criteria for evaluating different sight-singing collections provide a model that can be applied to any book or collection that a director is considering for use in instruction.

The first consideration in evaluating materials is the level of difficulty of the materials. Some books state the intended level, but the director must also check to see that the voice ranges and sequencing of materials will work for their particular ensemble. Most materials provide sight-singing examples that are graded for difficulty, but the author's expectations may differ from the students' abilities.

The next area of evaluation was content. Many of the questions regarding content came from the responses to the Web survey, and they highlight issues that concern the comprehensiveness of the musical examples. For instance, a surprising number of published materials only contain exercises written in treble clef despite the fact that at least one section in a mixed choir rarely reads in that clef. Some teachers prefer material that includes text or expressive markings and that offers both single-line and multipart exercises. *Correlated literature* refers to a practice more common

FIGURE 7.3. REVIEW FORM FOR CHORAL SIGHT-SINGING MATERIALS.

Sight-singing Review Form

Publication Information
  Title:
  Author:
  Publisher:
    Year of publication and purchase information

Organization and Content

Level and Sequence
  Beginning, intermediate, or advanced with appropriate voice ranges. Is the material graded (for difficulty) versus ungraded, # of examples?
Content
  a. Are exercises specially composed or drawn from existing literature?
  b. Are there separate pitch and rhythm exercises?
  c. Are some exercises in minor and other modes?
  d. Are exercises single-line, multipart, or both?
  e. Are exercises accompanied or unaccompanied?
  f. Are melodies written in both bass and treble clef?
  g. Do the exercises have text or expressive markings?
  h. Is there correlated literature—choral performance literature with pitch and rhythm content matched to the reading levels in the book?
Method
  Does the book follow a particular methodological approach or is it for general usage?
  Does it use a particular pitch or rhythm-reading system?
  Does it provide information and materials for teaching music fundamentals?
Evaluation
  Are evaluation materials or suggestions provided?
Distinguishing Features
  What are the strengths and weaknesses of the book?
  Is there information for the teacher regarding instructional strategies?
  Does the book come with any teaching/visual aids?
  Are other unique features or activities offered?

in instrumental method books. Correlated literature is literature for performance that corresponds to the students' skill level at that point in the sequence. So, for example, students who have completed a level 1 reading unit would have a piece that contained music they could sight-sing. Correlated literature helps students connect what they are learning in sight-singing to the literature they perform.

The questions under the "Method" section refer to the flexibility of using the book regardless of the sight-singing system used by the teacher. This section also asks whether or not the book provides ex-

amples of different reading systems and information on music fundamentals to complement the sight-singing practice.

The "Evaluation" section explores what materials or suggestions are
available to help the teacher track the students' progress. One of the
weaknesses of many of the commercially published sight-singing materials is a lack of information regarding assessment, particularly at the
individual level.

The final section covers any other distinguishing features that might
set a book apart from other available materials such as supplemental
materials, teaching tips, or musical activities. The materials are organized
alphabetically for ease of reference, and a summary chart (fig. 8.1) is provided at the end of the chapter so that teachers can quickly locate materials to fit specific needs.

8

Review of Materials

CHOIR TRAINER SERIES
Carl W. Vandre
Mills Music, Inc./CPP Belwin
Two-Part Choir Trainer (1956)	Student ($5.50)
SAB Choir Trainer (1956)	Student ($5.50)
The Four-Part Choir Trainer (1948)	Student ($5.50)

Level and Sequence: The ranges and difficulty of exercises could work for beginning middle school or high school, though part singing moves quickly. The book would be most appropriate for church choir or parochial school because of the sacred texts that accompany the song material. Exercises are graded in difficulty. Each book starts with the chord as "the basis of part singing." All three books go almost immediately to exercises for all parts, whether two, three, or four, and stay that way throughout. Exercises are not numbered or grouped by units in any way.

Content: All pieces and exercises are specially composed by Vandre. There are pitch drills to establish chord patterns and tonality but no rhythm-only drills. No minor melodies. Some unison exercises, but mostly in two to four parts, depending on the book. Some pieces are accompanied, some have reductions, and others are without piano parts at all. Drills have no text; all other examples have sacred texts. Two-part is all treble clef; the three- and four-part offer bass clef parts. Choral literature is provided in the book, with all pieces written by Vandre.

Method: Teachers could use either movable "do" or numbers for pitch reading, and both are provided underneath the warm-up exercises. Rhythm is handled very sporadically. In the two-part book, rhythms are presented based on "quarter note gets the beat," with no other meters represented. In the three-part book, rhythm is barely mentioned except when certain note values are introduced. The note values are not explained, just mentioned. At the beginning of the four-part book, there is a one-page explanation of a beat-based counting system that uses "down–up" for each quarter note: four quarters are spoken "down–down–down–down." There is very little music fundamentals information, and some of it is presented in a misleading way (e.g., "quarter note equals one beat"). New pitches or chords are mentioned when introduced, and the four-part book has a brief section on how to find "do."

Evaluation: No evaluation materials or suggestions. Vandre's approach is not really compatible with graded assessment because clear levels are not identified.

Distinguishing Features: Obviously, the inclusion of sacred texts limits the usefulness of the book for most public school settings today. The chordal approach seems well crafted and provides a solid introduction to part singing and traditional voice leading. The drills on chord tones and progressions are good "tune-up" exercises for a choir. Rhythm is virtually ignored and never complex. There is little information for the teacher on how to use the books.

CHORAL CONNECTIONS
Mollie Tower, Senior Ed.
Glencoe/McGraw-Hill (1999, 1997)

Mixed Voices, levels 1–4	Teacher ($28.80/ea); Student ($21.68); CDs ($12.98–$14.56/ea)
Resource Binder, levels 1–4	Teacher ($70.22/ea)
Male Voices, levels 1 and 3	Teacher ($28.80/ea); Student ($21.68); CDs ($12.98–$14.56/ea)
Treble Voices, level 1 and 3	Teacher ($28.80/ea); Student ($21.68); CDs ($12.98–$14.56/ea)

Level and Sequence: *Choral Connections* is a literature-based comprehensive choral curriculum that was designed to be used from middle school through high school level. It is included in this review because each lesson features preparatory material that involves rhythm drills, vocal warm-ups, and sight-singing that are tied to the piece for that lesson. Literature in the beginning levels (1 and 2) fits middle school choirs but could be used with a beginning high school choir with little choral background. The intermediate (3) and advanced (4) levels are recommended for high school. The intermediate level assumes some training and might be a difficult starting point musically for many beginning high school groups. While the books are identified by difficulty level, there is not a clear graded sequence from lesson to lesson as there might be in a stand-alone sight-singing book. Sequencing is up to the teacher, depending on the concepts or skills they wish to teach. Ranges usually fit changing voices in the early books.

Content: Each book includes "preparatory materials," which introduce musical fundamentals to help prepare students for sight-reading. Levels 1 and 2 start with the exact same material; levels 3 and 4 start with slightly more advanced versions of the same exercises. Each book has 14 to 16 literature-based lessons, which are designed to be taught over a period of time. Each lesson has teaching tips that guide the teacher from warm-ups through assessment and includes sight-singing and rhythmic exercises drawn from the literature for that lesson. While the lessons in each book are numbered, they are not ordered by difficulty and were not intended to be taught in order. This makes sense for a literature-based approach where programming would dictate some of the teacher's choices. The books also feature additional literature (24–29 total pieces/book) that comes with teaching tips but not the full-scale lesson. Several pieces in each book are presented in conjunction with more detailed information on the history of different periods in Western music and are coordinated with listening and integrated arts information.

Method: The book provides both movable "do" and movable numbers for pitch reading. Rhythm activities are designed to be clapped but could be chanted using any system. Musical terms and symbols are often presented as extension activities associated with the piece. Nice glossary of terms and symbols at the end of each book, along with a keyboard graphic. Lots of supplemental material and visual aids for teaching fundamentals in the teacher's resource binder.

Evaluation: Every lesson provides guidelines for student self-assessment, informal assessment, and formal assessment. The teacher's resource binder contains performance assessment criteria, rubrics, and guidelines for individual assessment procedures.

Distinguishing Features: This is an excellent collection of quality choral literature from a variety of historical and cultural traditions. The approach truly imbeds sight-singing within the process of learning literature for performance. The speed at which certain reading skills are presented might make it difficult to have *Choral Connections* as your only sight-singing resource. However, since the musical material in the literature is presented so clearly, the teacher could easily supplement students' training with exercises from other sources of comparable difficulty. Each book has the *National Standards* for music (either MS or HS) printed at the front of the text. Concepts and skills for each lesson are laid out at the beginning of each book and tied to the *National Standards*. A teacher could invest in a few of the manuals and accompanying binders and then purchase selected octavos separately for the students as they are programmed.

CHORAL READER
Maurice Gardner
Staff Music Publishing Company, Inc.
Treble Clef Voices (1977)   Student ($4.95)
Bass Clef Voices (1977)   Student ($4.95)

Level and Sequence: The material fits middle / junior high school ranges and skill levels. Exercises start with f as "do," so the ranges fit changing voices well. Exercises are graded in difficulty beginning with quarter notes and rests in $\frac{2}{4}$ time on "do" and "re." There are six units in the book, with 20 to 48 exercises of widely varying length per unit. The approach is scalar building, from "do" up to "sol" and then from "do" down to "sol."

Content: Exercises include some specially written ones but mostly familiar folk tunes and classical melodies. There are some separate rhythm "studies" and scales but mostly complete melodies. Minor mode appears with the introduction of accidentals in unit 6 and is introduced mainly through familiar melodies. Exercises are unison and two-part only, and melodies are presented mainly without text until unit 6. All melodies are unaccompanied and all in bass clef or treble clef, depending on the edition. Some two-part arrangements of familiar tunes, but no correlated literature.

Method: There is no specific method. The author uses "so-fa" syllables for pitch (movable "do") and supplements them occasionally with scale step numbers and pitch names. There is no syllable or counting system for rhythm, but many patterns are introduced by chanting on words. Unlike many books, *Choral Reader* supplies solfège syllables under the notes at the beginnings of exercises and in "tricky" places. Consequently, the book would not work well with a number or fixed "do" system. Musical concepts in the form of pitch and rhythm values or meter are introduced in the text but with little or no explanation. For example, on page 9 key signatures and two new notes are simultaneously introduced with no explanation.

Evaluation: No evaluation procedures are suggested, though the units could be used as benchmarks for teacher-designed assessment.

Distinguishing Features: Lots of familiar tunes are used. While some are specifically used for "Name That Tune" kinds of exercises, many are presented as sight-singing exercises. For example, exercise #37 on page 17 is titled "Round," but the melody is "Frère Jacques," which students would recognize shortly after beginning. However, singing solfège to familiar melodies is not a bad strategy for building aural pattern recognition. In general, the materials and the sequence seem dated and rely a great deal on the teacher to fill in the blanks.

ESSENTIAL MUSICIANSHIP
Emily Crocker and John Leavitt
Hal Leonard Corporation
Book 1 (1995)   Teacher ($19.95); Student ($9.95)
Book 2 (1995)   Teacher ($19.95); Student ($9.95)
Book 3 (1998)   Teacher ($19.95); Student ($9.95)

Level and Sequence: The series is designed to be used from middle school through high school level. Book 1 is designed for a beginning middle school choir (grades 7 and 8) but could be used with a beginning high school choir with little choral background. Book 2 is recommended for grades 9 and 10 and might be a better starting point for many beginning high school groups. Book 3 is recommended for grades 11 and 12 (provided they have had prior training) and is thus more advanced, beginning with a review of all the minor keys and an introduction to the entire circle of fifths. Ranges usually fit changing voices in the early book, and the teaching tips identify places where ranges may have to be altered.

Content: *Essential Musicianship* is not just a sight-singing book but also a comprehensive choral method that includes vocal training, music theory (fundamentals), sight reading, and performance. It is similar in structure to instrumental method books that combine the development of playing skills with music reading and fundamentals. The sight-singing content begins with separate pitch and rhythm drills in book 1. The layout is similar to the *Patterns of Sound* approach, with combinable unison lines for early two-part singing, but the content moves more quickly. By unit 5 pitch and rhythm practice are combined. Early performance pieces are "Speech Choruses" that focus on diction and rhythm. Unit 5 offers a sung unison performance piece in the range of a fifth accompanied, but the book moves to simple four-part a cappella by unit 6. Both clefs are presented from the beginning. Nice balance of exercises and pieces with text. Almost all of the literature in the series is by Crocker and Leavitt, two very well established composers of school choral music, but there is an accompanying *Essential Repertoire* series available in treble, male, or mixed editions that offers a broader selection of correlated literature at four different levels.

Method: While rooted in a sound-before-symbol approach, the series takes pains not to be system-specific with regard to pitch or rhythm, and many of the contributing teachers use different systems. The appendix offers a very thorough overview of the major pitch and rhythm syllable systems as well as extra pitch and rhythm drills. New music theory information is presented in each unit to accompany the sight-reading exercises. The theory information is carefully sequenced using a scale approach, with lots of visual aids and information for the teacher on how to present it.

Evaluation: Evaluation opportunities are presented in the form of review chapters for theory and sight reading. They include questions about content such as, "What is a clef?" and symbol identification that could be presented to the group or in the form of individual tests. No guidelines for sight-singing skill tests are provided, but the material could easily be adapted for any of the testing procedures given in chapter 6 of this book.

Distinguishing Features: Almost too many to name. Has the *National Standards* for music printed at the front of the text. Goals and objectives for each unit are stated at the beginning and are tied to the standards. Each book is clearly laid out in 20 units, with the musical content specified in the table of contents. A wealth of information on good teaching practice throughout all of the books. Lots of supplemental materials and very easy to use. An outstanding choral curriculum if you can afford it.

THE FOLK SONG SIGHT SINGING SERIES
Edgar Crowe, Annie Lawton, and W. Gillies Whittaker, Eds.
Oxford University Press

Books 1 and 3 (1933/1961)	Student ($3.50)
Books 2, 4, and 5 (1933/1961)	Student ($4.50)
Books 6–10 (1933/1961)	Student ($5.50)

Level and Sequence: The series can be used from elementary school through college, though the small size of the books (and the print) probably makes them better suited for older students. Eight hundred and thirty-four folk tunes are carefully sequenced from book 1 through book 10, so that each new section of folk melodies introduces only one new pitch or rhythm challenge. The material is sequenced by interval content, harmonic outlines, modes, accidentals, and metric challenges up through book 8. Books 9 and 10 provide two-part folk tunes with descants.

Content: The content is drawn entirely from the folk repertoire, and the origins of every tune are given. There are no "exercises" per se, only the folk melodies themselves. Expressive markings such as phrases and dynamics have been added and all texts removed. Minor mode is introduced in book 2 and appears in sections of every book from then on. All exercises are unaccompanied unison melodies written in treble clef.

Method: A concise but informative discussion of method at the beginning of each book suggests the use of "solfa," a form of movable "do" with minor "la." The first 50 exercises in book 1 identify the location of "do" for the student. No rhythm system is offered, though "time names" are mentioned, suggesting the Curwen system. The material could be used with any pitch- or rhythm-reading system. No theory information is offered except to identify the musical content being introduced in the next set of melodies.

Evaluation: No evaluation materials or suggestions are included. The books themselves indicate levels of achievement, but within each book levels would have to be determined by the teacher.

Distinguishing Features: The books in this popular series contain between 50 and 110 folk melodies each, sequenced according to difficulty, for a relatively inexpensive price. The fact that all of the tunes are drawn from existing folk music instead of being specially composed adds to their validity for sight-singing practice. The books are small in size, which sometimes makes the notation a challenge to read but allows them to fit easily in a choir folder. The biggest weakness is the lack of bass clef examples. If the books were reissued in a slightly larger size with bigger print, more modern typesetting, and a variety of clefs, they would be even more valuable.

Related Oxford Sight-Singing Books
Sing at Sight, William Appleby ($5.00)
Sing in Harmony, William Appleby ($7.95)
Firsts & Seconds, William Appleby and Frederick Fowler ($5.00)
Seconds & Thirds / More Seconds and Thirds, Kenneth Pont ($5.00)

THE INDEPENDENT SINGER
Richard Edstrom
Curtis Music Press (1978)
Complete kit ($23.50), including teacher's manual and reproducible student exercises

---

Level and Sequence: The book is designed for upper-level junior high and beginning high school choirs, though ranges as written are sometimes too wide for changing voices. The exercises are graded for difficulty, beginning with examples that have no key or meter, just an identified pulse. There are 59 sets of three exercises each. The author recommends singing 1 set per day only. Beginning with exercise 20, the interval content becomes an organizing feature, starting with seconds and thirds and gradually widening. Familiar tunes such as "My Bonnie Lies over the Ocean" are used to introduce the sound of a new interval both ascending and descending.

Content: Most exercises are specially composed, though the author throws in a classical or folk tune from time to time. All of the exercises feature both pitch and rhythm content, though key signatures do not appear until exercise #13 with G major and meter signatures are not introduced until exercise #28. All exercises are in major, though accidentals are introduced in exercise #51. Exercises are mostly unison, with four-part exercises being introduced in exercise #43 and no two- or three-part exercises. All exercises are unaccompanied and the author uses both treble and bass clef from the beginning. Recommended tempos for the beat value are given throughout, but no other expressive markings are present. None of the exercises have text, and there is no correlated literature.

Method: Both movable "do" and numbers are written with the scale, but the reading procedure refers to identifying "do" for each key in which one reads. No specific rhythm-reading system is suggested, though counts are recommended starting in exercise #28 as meter is introduced. Until that point the student is told what value gets the beat and determines its mathematical relationship to the other time values. Theory information is carefully sequenced throughout the text in relation to the new singing material being introduced. The only exception is found at the beginning of the book, where an entire unit is devoted to pitch names on the grand staff and a second unit to rhythm names and their relational time values. This is all done prior to the first singing exercise in a symbol-before-sound approach, though the teacher could choose to introduce this information more gradually.

Evaluation: The book features review tests throughout on the theoretical information and reading procedures that have been introduced. No singing tests are suggested.

Distinguishing Features: From the very beginning the author is careful that students do not associate the idea of "beat" only with quarter notes or "do" only with c. The author encourages teaching students a five-point reading procedure to identify the clef, key, location of "do," starting pitch (syllable), and meter. The teacher's manual comes in a kit with reproducible sheets for the students. For $23.50 the teacher has permission to make an unlimited number of copies for the students. The book's approach is very simple tonally, with a lot of stepwise writing and gradual interval introduction. The approach to rhythm is designed to keep the student flexible with regard to meter/beat associations. Thus when meter is finally introduced, it constantly shifts between quarter-, half-, and eighth-note bases. Accidentals are introduced without any corresponding solfège syllables in exercise #51, with some very challenging examples.

INTRODUCTION TO SIGHT-SINGING AND THE CHORAL SIGHT SINGER
Stanley Arkis and Herman Schuckman
Carl Fischer

Volume 1: *Introduction to Sight-Singing* (1968)	Student ($7.95)
Volume 2: *The Choral Sight Singer* (1970)	Student ($4.95)

Level and Sequence: Volume 1 is intended for the musical beginner, but the ranges and speed with which it moves suggest an older beginner, such as someone beginning in high school or church choir. Volume 2 picks up at the end of volume 1 and moves even faster. The material could even be appropriate for beginning university students. Exercises are graded and start with do-sol in stepwise movement and then add scale tones and interval skips. Each lesson introduces at least one and often two new concepts, and the lessons move rather quickly. Anywhere from five to nine exercises per lesson.

Content: Volume 1 uses some folk and art music melodies along with specially composed tunes. Volume 2 seems to be mostly specially composed pieces supposedly written in Baroque, Classical, Romantic, and Modern styles to emphasize an artistic approach to reading. However, few of the exercises have a text or any expressive markings beyond tempo, and dynamics are entirely absent. Volume 2 introduces minor keys and mixed meters by lessons 5 and 6. By the end of the volume, the exercises cover chromaticism and irregular meters and are quite challenging. Volume 1 is all unison in treble clef, while volume 2 offers both treble and bass clef and exercises in unison to three parts. All exercises are unaccompanied, and no correlated choral literature accompanies the series.

Method: The books use a movable "do" system with either "la-" or "do-" based minor for pitch reading and a measure-based counting system for rhythm. In volume 1, the authors begin with a page of pitch and rhythm patterns that they recommend teaching by rote followed by teaching students the elements of musical notation, which include the staff, both clefs, note names, $\frac{2}{4}$, $\frac{3}{4}$, $\frac{4}{4}$, and $\frac{6}{8}$ and all the note values based on quarter gets a beat. The authors mention in volume 2 that a teacher may wish to use another system, but they begin some exercises with the movable solfège syllables written underneath, which would make it difficult to use the book any other way. There is an overview of musical elements at the beginning of volume 1 and then a brief presentation of new material before each lesson.

Evaluation: No evaluation materials are given, but volume 2's lesson 25 is labeled "Test of Musicianship" and includes modulating melodies, chromaticism, meters and rhythms, and intervals. It is all in unison, so it may be intended as an individualized test. No information is given on how to use it.

Distinguishing Features: Both volumes begin with a preface that lays out the content and recommendations for teaching. Though carefully sequenced in difficulty, the material is very challenging, especially in *The Choral Sight Singer*. The books move very quickly, without a great deal of review. A good choice for a more mature choir.

JENSON SIGHT SINGING COURSE
David Bauguess
Jenson Publications/Hal Leonard Corporation
Volume 1 (1984)   Teacher ($19.95); Student ($2.50);
                     Introductory Cassette ($9.95); Demonstration Cassette
                     ($14.95)
Volume 2 (1985)   Teacher ($19.95); Student ($2.50)

Level and Sequence: The course is intended for beginning-level singers from seventh grade through high school. Ranges are fairly limited in both bass and treble clef, though high school boys would have an easier time with the bass lines. However, the movable tonic allows the teacher to move keys as needed. The two volumes contain 578 graded exercises divided into 14 levels of difficulty. For each level new rhythms are introduced first by themselves followed by pitch exercises that utilize the rhythmic material. It is carefully sequenced according to pitch, rhythm, and conceptual information. All of the elements at each level are summarized in Appendix A, so that the teacher can identify where students are at any point.

Content: While some familiar folk melodies are used, almost all of the exercises are specially composed according to the pitch and rhythm content of the sequence. No attempt is made to connect the exercises to literature. Rhythm exercises are used to introduce new note values or meters, but elements like syncopation are introduced within a pitch exercise context. All of the exercises are unaccompanied. Volume 1 exercises are all in major keys. Volume 2 begins with level 10 and introduces three chromatic tones. Minor melodies are not introduced until level 13, when all three forms of the minor scale are presented. Volume 1 begins with single-line reading and then adds a second part in exercise 78. Three- and four-part exercises are eventually added. Clefs are not used in the notation or introduced until exercise 126 (level 4), at which time both treble and bass clefs are introduced. Key signatures are introduced in exercise 95 but without clefs, though all melodies are notated as if in treble clef.

Method: The series advocates movable "do" solfège and includes the syllables in the teacher's manual. Numbers are included parenthetically for the first nine levels. Rhythm is taught using counting. A lot of information is given in the teacher's edition for presenting music fundamentals. New terms and concepts are highlighted at each level and explanations given for the teacher to use. How much theoretical information is communicated to the students is left somewhat up to the teacher's discretion.

Evaluation: The level system provides a nice framework for a teacher interested in evaluating progress. No tests are included as part of the series, but the clear description of skills and content at each level allows test exercises to be constructed very easily.

Distinguishing Features: In the teacher's edition, teaching tips, solfège and rhythm syllables, and theoretical information accompany the exercises. A seven-page introduction to volume 1 details how the author believes the series can best be used, from reading procedures to pep talks. The series is somewhat mechanical, and while the occasional familiar tune is thrown in, the emphasis is on reading practice through exercises, not music. The lack of clefs or key signatures at the beginning of exercises, while intended to simplify, makes the exercises seem even more removed from real music. On the plus side, the early introduction of bass clef and the constant shifting of meters and keys throughout the exercises build the students' flexibility in applying solfège and rhythm reading to different contexts. While the series is very well organized in terms of scope and sequence, the teacher's edition does not reference pages or displays in the student book, so one must always have both books on hand to prepare instruction. An outstanding feature is Appendix C in volume 2, which offers a listing of octavos for sight-singing organized from level 4 (one piece) through level 14. The octavos are further divided by unison, two-part, male or female voicing, and mixed voicing, as well as by difficulty levels (easy, medium, and hard).

THE KEYS TO SIGHT READING SUCCESS
John Hemmenway, Mary Belle Leach, Mary Nan Wehrung, and Marsha Carlisle
AMC Publications, a division of Alliance Music Publishers

Book 1: *Introduction to Sight Reading* (1977)	Student ($2.95)
Book 2: *50 Easy Four-Part Exercises* (1983)	Student ($2.95)
Book 3: *125 Moderate Two-Part Exercises*	
Treble Clef (1987)	Student ($3.25)
Bass Clef (1988)	Student ($3.25)
Book 4: *90 Easy Three-Part Exercises* (1991)	Student ($6.95)

Level and Sequence: Intended for beginning choirs from middle school on up. Ranges would work with middle school singers. Book 1 contains 30 graded lessons, with a number of exercises per lesson. The rest of the books state the number of exercises in the title. Book 1 is a predecessor to book 2, but books 3 and 4 are intended to stand alone. All books are graded by difficulty.

Content: All exercises are specially composed for the series. None of the exercises feature text (except for three rhythm chants in book 1) or expressive markings. Book 1 is correlated with book 1 of the Oxford *Folk Song Sight Singing Series*. For each lesson the authors have given corresponding Oxford examples for extra practice. Book 1 contains mostly unison melodies but does offer an introduction to simple two- and three-part singing, all in treble clef. Book 2 is standard four-part voicing using tenor-treble clef. Book 3 is sold in a treble and bass clef version. Book 4 offers SSA and SAB voicings of identical exercises on facing pages. Minor first appears in exercise #37 of book 2, and minor exercises are very sparse in books 3 and 4. All of the exercises are unaccompanied.

Method: The authors specify movable "do" or numbers for pitch reading in book 1 only and offer exercises with the solfège syllables and numbers indicated. The subsequent books could be used with any system. No rhythm system is indicated or recommended. No information on music fundamentals is given.

Evaluation: No guidelines or recommendations for evaluation are given. The organization does not lend itself well to regular individual assessment.

Distinguishing Features: Since the books were written progressively over a period of time, there is some unevenness in presentation. None of the books contain any visual aids or music fundamentals information, and they offer little in the way of teaching tips. Book 1 simply outlines the lessons by content, while book 2 gives a cursory overview of the contents and a couple of teaching recommendations in the foreword. Book 3 offers some teaching tips but outlines the lessons only by rhythm content and keys. The cost of books 1–3 makes them attractive as a source of supplemental exercises written in one to four parts.

KODÀLY CHORAL METHOD (BRITISH EDITION)	
Zoltàn Kodàly Percy M. Young, Ed.	
Boosey & Hawkes	
333 Elementary Exercises (1963)	Student ($6.50)
50 Nursery Songs within the Range of Five Notes (1964)	Student ($15.95)
Bicinia Hungarica I–IV: 180 Progressive Two-Part Songs (1962)	Student ($5.95–$8.95)
Five volumes of *Two-Part* Exercises (1964)	Student ($5.00–$13.50)
Tricinia Hungarica: 29 Progressive Three-Part Songs (1964)	Student ($12.50)
Let Us Sing Correctly: 101 Exercises in Intonation (1952)	Student ($6.95)
Fifteen Two-Part Exercises (1965)	Student ($6.25)

Level and Sequence: These books of exercises can be used for sight-singing training from elementary through high school level (and even at the university). Carefully sequenced musical material that builds a student's tonal and rhythmic vocabulary is at the heart of the Kodàly approach to teaching. All of the books are British editions of the exercises and folk song arrangements that Kodàly wrote for use in the Hungarian school system.

Content: The sequence begins with 333 elementary exercises, which are all about eight measures long, without text, and in treble clef. Some exercises give the starting syllable, and only a few give dynamics and phrase markings, though the foreword encourages the teacher to assign dynamics and to avoid "expressionless singing." *Let Us Sing Correctly* offers short two-part exercises without text to be sung on solfège. Their primary purpose is to drill good intonation with exercises that outline different triadic functions. All exercises are unaccompanied in treble clef using pentatonic, major, and minor scales.

The two-part songs in *Bicinia Hungarica* written or arranged by Kodàly, are all offered with texts and expressive markings. The pitch material is carefully graded, with lots of imitation between voices. The rhythmic challenges are considerable, in part because they are idiomatic to Hungarian folk music with "snap" figures (♪♩.) and mixed meters. Pentatonic, major, and minor modalities are used. The *Tricinia* is only one volume of three-part pieces without text, though all examples have full expressive markings.

Method: The books are designed to be used with the *Kodàly Choral Method*, which involves using movable "do" solfège, la-based minor, Curwen hand signs, and Kodàly's beat-based rhythm syllables (though no notes on rhythm syllables or rhythm instruction is given). Limited teaching information is given; however, forewords by Kodàly in *Let Us Sing Correctly* and *Bicinia Hungarica* are interesting to read. No theory information is provided, but good notes are given on the pitch and rhythm content of the various exercises and songs in each sequence.

Evaluation: No evaluation materials or recommendations are given.

Distinguishing Features: The *Kodàly Choral Method* has a great deal of credibility with music educators due to its remarkable success in teaching Hungarian students to read music. It is difficult to know how much of that success is attributable to Kodàly's teaching method and how much to a national curriculum that was consistently and universally taught over a number of years. The material is based in Hungarian folk music in order to build on Hungarian children's existing musical vocabulary. Consequently, it is somewhat less suited to American children's musical experiences. One weakness is that all of the music is presented in treble clef, even the three-part songs. Since this is a British edition, rhythm is presented as crochets and quavers.

NOTE: The following books (also published by Boosey) are based on the Kodàly concept but feature material more geared toward American students:

Szönyi, E., *Bicinia Americana, vol. 1: 22 Traditional American Children's Songs*.

Tacka, P., and M. Houlahan, *Sound Thinking*, vols. 1 and 2: *Sight Singing*.

MASTERWORKS SIGHT-SINGING COLLECTION
(all series available in SATB, SSAA, or TTBB voicing)
The Renaissance Sight-Singing Series
Edward DeNardis
Volumes 1–5   ($35.00 each)

The Baroque Sight-Singing Series
Nicholas Palmer
Volumes I–5   ($35.00 each)

The Classical Sight-Singing Series
Hank Beebe
Volumes 1–5   ($35.00 each)

The Romantic Sight-Singing Series
Hank Beebe
Volumes 1–5   ($35.00 each)

The Easy Rhythm Sight-Singing Series
Hank Beebe
(also sold as *The Cambiata Sight-Singing Series*)   ($35.00 each) (voicing SA(T)B,
Volumes 1–5   SAB, SSA, TTB, TBB)

Level and Sequence: The books are designed for high school level and
above and represent one of the more challenging sets of material on the
market today. The ranges require more mature voices with basses needing a low f even in volume 1. Each series is organized by difficulty based
solely on interval content beginning with stepwise part writing and adding wider intervals as the volumes progress. The *Romantic* series begins
with leaps up to a sixth and then progresses in difficulty by adding chromatic pitches.

The rhythmic content of each series is quite challenging even in volume 1. The exception is the *Easy Rhythm* series, designed for beginning
choirs, which carefully sequences content according to rhythmic difficulty. Each volume contains 30 one-page compositions.

Content: The Masterworks concept is to provide original choral material for sight-singing written in the style of different historical periods.
The publisher thinks that this provides students with a more authentic
and musical reading experience. All the exercises are specially composed,
but attempt to replicate the compositional styles of different historical
periods. All of the exercises are four-part (three-part in the *Easy Rhythm*
series), unaccompanied choral scores and can be purchased in a wide
variety of voicings depending on the teacher's needs. They feature a
variety of meters including $\frac{2}{4}$ (cut time), $\frac{3}{4}$, $\frac{4}{4}$, and $\frac{6}{8}$ from volume 1 on (with
the exception of the *Renaissance* series, which stays mostly in $\frac{4}{4}$), but no
mixed or irregular meters. The exercises are primarily in major but feature common modulations such as secondary dominants and relative
minor as early as the first exercise of volume 1. Minor mode appears in

volume 1 of every series and as early as exercise 2 in the *Renaissance* and *Classical* series and exercise 3 in the *Romantic* series. Even in the simpler Easy Rhythm series, minor mode and accidentals are introduced early in volume 1. Chromatic pitches are common in the *Romantic* series and progress from stepwise chromaticism in volume 1 to chromatic leaps in the later volumes.

None of the exercises have text and there are surprisingly few expressive markings. While one might understand the lack of dynamic or expressive markings in the Renaissance series, they are also absent in the Baroque series. The classical series adds some articulation and tempo markings such as ritardando, but still doesn't specify dynamic levels. The Romantic series finally adds dynamics, but with few gradual dynamic changes indicated. There is no literature associated with the exercises in the books, though Masterworks also publishes a *Sight-Singing with Words* series, an *Easy Reading Concert Series*, and a number of public domain octavos (see later).

Method: The exercises in the Masterworks series were designed to be used with movable "do" and are therefore written in a variety of keys that could be challenging for fixed "do" classes but shouldn't present a problem for numbers users. The first page in volume 1 of each series gives information on how to sing altered syllables and some warm-up exercises with the movable "do" syllables (except in the *Romantic* series, which has more detailed information on altered solfège syllables but no warm-up exercises).

No system for rhythm-reading is recommended in any of the series, though the authors suggest starting students on *Melodia* if they aren't prepared to read the rhythms in the *Masterworks* exercises. This suggestion is given even in the beginning of *Easy Rhythm* series, which one would think was designed to prepare rhythm reading.

Evaluation: The organization of each series into levels provides a nice framework for a teacher interested in evaluating progress. No tests are included as part of the series, but the clear description of content at each level would allow test exercises to be constructed or pulled from the material very easily.

Distinguishing Features: The primary benefit of the Masterworks series is that you buy each volume only once and then have unlimited photocopying permission. Thus an initial investment of $175.00 for a complete single-copy set of any series would provide materials for a lifetime. The books give very little in the way of teaching aids; they are primarily intended as sets of materials. All of the exercises have measure numbers, which is a real plus for working through reading challenges with a group. The biggest drawback to the books is the high level of rhythmic challenge in a four-part context. However, some teachers, tired of the simplistic quarter-note songs of many books, may see this as a strength. *Masterworks* provides a variety of engaging and challenging materials for a more advanced group, but students should have a good command of basic pitch and rhythm reading before starting on this series. Some of the other publications from this company seem to be geared toward a more beginning level sight reader.

The following series are also available from Masterworks Press:

Sight-Singing with Words
Hank Beebe
Volumes 1–3 ($50.00 each)
 Original tunes for sight-singing but with texts from the "great poets."

Steps to Harmony
Nicholas Palmer
Volumes 1–5 ($35.00 each)
 Designed for middle school through college. Three-part exercises that can be sung together or separately with limited ranges and simpler rhythms (though they get complicated rather quickly). Available in treble or bass clef.

371 Bach Chorales
Volumes 1–4 ($50.00 each)
 This wonderful collection provides teachers with these classic chorale materials in open score, organized by difficulty, with measure numbers and easily reproducible. A separate book containing a complete set of piano reductions is also available ($12.00).

MELODIA: A COMPREHENSIVE COURSE IN SIGHT-SINGING
Samuel W. Cole and Leo R. Lewis
Oliver Ditson Company (1909)

Book I	$3.95
Book II	$4.00
Books I–IV (single volume)	$8.95

Level and Sequence: The authors write that *Melodia* is intended for "use in conservatories and by private teachers." However, the material begins at a fairly basic level, and book 1 could be used with beginners in junior high or high school and book 2 with more advanced singers who are approaching collegiate level. The range of many exercises spans at least an octave, which probably makes *Melodia* a better choice for high school age singers and above. The four books contain 1,508 graded exercises divided into 11 levels of difficulty, called series. The approach is interval-based rather than scale-based, with accidentals and leaps being sequenced according to harmonic functions. The approach is carefully sequenced but moves very quickly into challenging rhythms, intervals, and meters.

Content: The musical material is evenly divided between melodies taken from existing works of classical composers from Bach to Wagner and specially composed exercises. As the material becomes more challenging, more excerpts from existing pieces are used. All of the exercises feature both pitch and rhythm content and are fully notated with key and meter signatures from the beginning. The book opens with exercises in C major written in treble clef. Bass clef is introduced in exercise #206 and then alternates with treble on a regular basis. Book 2 begins with series 3, which introduces accidentals along with shifts to the relative minor. The exercises get challenging quickly, and by the end of book 2 students have read melodies in all keys and in a variety of meters from $\frac{2}{2}$ to $\frac{3}{8}$ with all diatonic intervals and a number of chromatic alterations. Two-part exercises are introduced in book 2, series 4, and are also presented in series 6, series 8, series 10, and series 11. From book 3 onward the exercises feature more excerpts from existing music, including many difficult contrapuntal examples and chromatic melodies.

Method: No recommendations for pitch or rhythm reading are given. No music theory information is included. This is strictly a collection of exercises that could be used with any approach.

Evaluation: There are no recommended procedures or materials for evaluation, but the structure of each book offers opportunities to assess students as they move from one series to the next.

Distinguishing Features: *Melodia* is the oldest sight-singing book presented here, but it is still in print and, as the survey indicated, is still in use in some schools. Part of the reason for its longevity may be the sheer number of exercises included for a relatively modest price. This leads to one quirk of the book. To save space, exercises are laid out end to end so that an exercise can begin in the middle of a line. This can be difficult to follow in part because if the key does not change between two exercises on the same line, the key signature is not renotated at the beginning of the exercise. Thus a student often has to be careful to look all the way back to the beginning of the line for the key of the exercise. *Melodia* is an economical source of numerous graded exercises.

MUSIC READING UNLIMITED
Vivian Munn
Southern Music Company
Level 1 (1997)   Teacher ($39.95); Student ($9.95)
Level 2 (1998)   Teacher ($39.95); Student ($9.95)

Level and Sequence: The books are designed for a relatively advanced high school choir. Each book is clearly organized into 11 units, and the first unit in each book is a review. Book 1 assumes that students can already read basic time values in simple meters, keys with two sharps or flats, and simple four-part exercises built on I, IV, and V7. Each unit introduces new rhythmic/metric and pitch/key content, with anywhere from 10 to 31 exercises per unit. The approach to choral reading is harmonically based.

Content: All exercises appear to be specially composed for the series to reflect the specific musical content. There are no dynamics or other expressive markings of any kind for any of the examples in the entire series. New rhythmic material is introduced via rhythm-only exercises, but all pitch material is presented in a rhythmic context. Natural and harmonic minor keys are introduced in level 1, unit 10. Exercises are written in unison (though written in both octaves on the grand staff), two-part (written in four staves), and four-part in every unit. The four-part exercises offer piano reductions "as an aid to the teacher," but they are not to be played during reading. Treble and bass clefs are used from the very beginning. None of the exercises have texts, and there is no correlated literature.

Method: While the books are not entirely method-specific, the exercises are designed to be used with a "tonality-centered" approach to pitch reading such as movable "do" or movable numbers. The author offers her own "hybrid movable number" system, which uses numbers for scale steps and syllables ("ti," "fi," "te") for accidentals. The book uses "la-" or "6"-based minor. The author recommends a measure-based counting system for rhythm (1 & 2 &, etc.). Theory is presented through the musical content of the exercises, with limited theoretical information provided in the student books.

Evaluation: There are clear divisions into units, which would facilitate teacher-designed assessments, but no recommendations or materials for assessment are provided.

Distinguishing Features: The teacher's manual has a spiral binding to enable it to lie flat on a stand or piano. All the exercises are on the right-hand pages, with teaching tips on the facing left-hand pages so that the pages of the teacher's guide match the pages in the student books. This is helpful because each unit begins with exercise #1 instead of having continuous numbering throughout the book and there is no unit number identified on the exercise or the page header. The introduction to both books outlines the content of the entire series very clearly, so that teachers could skip around (though it is not encouraged). This is one of the most advanced sight-singing series in terms of content. While there are a limited number of examples for practice at each level of content, the author states that the exercises are "music reading studies, rather than sight-reading drills" to be studied and practiced to mastery.

PATTERNS OF SOUND
Joyce Eilers Bacak and Emily Crocker
Jenson Publications/Hal Leonard Corporation
Volume 1 (1988)   Teacher ($14.95); Student ($2.95); Cassette ($20.00)
Volume 2 (1989)   Teacher ($14.95); Student ($3.50); Cassette ($20.00)

Level and Sequence: The books are intended for beginning level and are appropriate for upper elementary school. The difficulty level could also fit beginning middle school, but the writing is all for equal-voiced treble. The ranges are limited enough in much of the part singing to accommodate middle school boys singing down the octave. Pitch routine #1 has do-sol in simple unison patterns that can immediately combine to do two-part singing. The exercises are graded with literature appropriate to the reading level included in the books. Volume 1 ends with a "real" two-part song.

Content: The exercises in both volumes were composed for the book, and all of the pieces in volume 1 were specially written. The exercises and song material move from more separate pitch and rhythm exercises to much more integrated exercise material. The pitch routines always include whatever rhythms have been introduced, and volume 2 integrates practice much more into a literature and part-singing context. Both volumes feature only treble clef and primarily equal-voiced music. Volume 2 contains more traditional canons or settings of folk songs, such as "Ezekiel Saw the Wheel," "Home on the Range," and so forth. Since both of the authors also compose and arrange choral music professionally, the settings are a cut above. Minor melodies and accidentals come only near the end of volume 2. Exercises and some two-part songs are unaccompanied, but most of the pieces have accompaniments. Good balance of text and no-text examples to sing. The pieces within the collection are a form of correlated literature, but there are also octavos called "Patterns in Performance" that are chosen to accompany the series.

Method: The authors are both trained in the Kodály method, and the rhythm syllables and movable "do" solfège reflect that orientation. The sequence also follows a sound-before-symbol approach in terms of students learning terminology for things after having reading experiences. For example, "How to Find 'Do,'" an introduction to key signatures, does not appear until page 49 of volume 2 even though students have been reading solfège in many keys up to this point. There is an excellent glossary of musical terms and symbols at the end of volume 2. Music theory information such as key signatures, time signatures, and accidentals is always introduced in the context of reading procedures.

Evaluation: There is no information regarding levels of achievement within each volume. No assessment guidelines or assessment materials are offered.

Distinguishing Features: The organization of the series is logical and very musical. Several unique features, including "Let's Harmonize" sections, where single-line melodies can be combined into two or more parts, and "Name That Tune," where students must sound out and identify familiar tunes from notation. Ranges and style of materials best suited to young treble groups (no bass clef) but could work for other beginning ensembles. The teacher's edition offers teaching tips for every exercise or song.

PATTERNS OF SOUND SERIES: THE CHORAL APPROACH TO SIGHT SINGING
Emily Crocker and Joyce Eilers
Jenson Publications/Hal Leonard Corporation
Volume 1 (1990)   Teacher ($19.95); Student ($17.50 for 5-pack);
                  Cassette ($25.00)
Volume 2 (1990)   Teacher ($19.95); Student ($17.50 for 5-pack);
                  Cassette ($25.00)

Level and Sequence: This second two-volume collection in the *Patterns of Sound Series* is designed especially for middle school mixed choir. The ranges of the boys' parts stay within the sixth between f below middle c and d above. Unlike the original series, both treble and bass clef are used from the very beginning. The approach and layout is very similar to that of the original *Patterns of Sound*, but this series moves a little more quickly. The authors suggest that *Choral Approach* could be used either as a follow up to the *Patterns* books or as a beginning-level book starting at square one. The latter seems more likely, since although it moves a little more quickly, it covers much of the same ground as the earlier book. Volume 2 of *Choral Approach* could be used as the next step after volume 2 of *Patterns*. Exercises and song material are interspersed throughout the book. By pitch exercise 4 in volume 1, the lines can be combined into a three-part texture, which remains throughout the rest of the books. Volume 1 ends by introducing the keys up to four flats and three sharps, while rhythmic difficulty does not go beyond eighth notes, simple meters, and dotted rhythms. Volume 2 adds more rhythmic complexity and introduces accidentals and minor mode about two-thirds of the way into the book.

Content: The exercises in both volumes were composed for the book, and all of the pieces (12 in volume 1, 14 in volume 2) were probably written or arranged just for the book. Since both of the authors also compose and arrange choral music professionally, the settings are a cut above.

Eight of the 12 pieces in volume 1 are accompanied, and all of the pieces in volume 2 are accompanied. All of the exercises are unaccompanied. The accompanied pieces within the collection are a form of correlated literature. They are definitely suitable for performance if desired.

Method: The authors are both trained in the Kodàly method, and the rhythm syllables and use of movable "do"/minor "la" solfège reflect that orientation. There is an excellent section called "Terms and Symbols" and a glossary of musical terms, but only at the end of the teacher's editions, not the student books. Music theory information such as key signatures, time signatures, and accidentals is always introduced in the context of reading procedures.

Evaluation: There is no information regarding levels of achievement within each volume. No assessment guidelines or assessment materials are offered.

Distinguishing Features: Very musical, like the earlier *Patterns* books. Good balance of text and no-text examples to sing. Features more of the "Let's Harmonize" and "Name That Tune" sections. Perfect for middle school mixed choir in both difficulty and range. The teacher's edition offers teaching tips for every exercise or song.

PATTERNS OF SOUND SERIES: SIGHT-SINGING FOR SSA
Emily Crocker and Joyce Eilers
Jenson Publications/Hal Leonard Corporation (1994)
Teacher ($14.95); Student ($3.50)

Level and Sequence: This addition to the *Patterns of Sound Series* is designed especially for beginning to intermediate SSA choirs. The approach and layout are very similar to the original *Patterns of Sound*, but this book moves much more quickly. For example, page 21 of the student book features a three-part a cappella piece. *Sight-Singing for SSA* would be a logical continuation of the *Patterns* series for a middle school treble group (though it reviews many of the same musical concepts) but could also work as a starter book for an older group. Exercises and song material are interspersed throughout the book. The book ends with rather quick coverage of $\frac{6}{8}$ meter, accidentals, minor keys, and modulation.

Content: The exercises in both volumes were composed for the book, and all of the pieces (18) were probably written or arranged just for the book but might be sold separately. Since both of the authors also compose and arrange choral music professionally, the settings are a cut above. All of the exercises are unaccompanied, as are 13 of the 18 pieces. The pieces are suitable for performance if desired, though some are very short.

Method: The authors are both trained in the Kodàly method, and the rhythm syllables and use of movable "do"/minor "la" solfège reflect that orientation. Music theory information such as key signatures, time signatures, and accidentals is always introduced in the context of reading procedures. No glossary of terms and symbols at the end.

Evaluation: There is no information regarding levels of achievement, and no assessment guidelines or assessment materials are offered.

Distinguishing Features: Very musical, like the earlier *Patterns* books. Features more of the "Let's Harmonize" and "Name That Tune" sections. Perfect for a more advanced middle school treble choir in both difficulty and range. The teacher's edition offers teaching tips for every exercise or song.

SIGHT READING FUN SERIES
Carl W. Vandre
Belwin-Mills

Sing or Play Sight Reading Fun—Unison (1956)	Student ($4.50)
Two-Part Sight Reading Fun—Treble (1940)	Student ($5.00)
Three-Part Sight Reading Fun—SSA (1940)	Student ($4.00)
Sight Reading Fun for Changed Voices—TTBB (1942)	Student ($4.00)
SAB Sight Reading Fun (1956)	Student ($4.50)
Four-Part Sight Reading Fun—SATB (1940)	Student ($4.50)

Level and Sequence: The series spans elementary through high school level, with careful attention to moderate ranges for middle school singers. Exercises are graded in difficulty. The unison book starts with scalar exercises, while the part books use a more chordal approach as "the basis of part singing." All books go almost immediately to exercises for the appropriate number of parts, whether two, three, or four, and stay that way throughout. Exercises are not numbered or grouped by level.

Content: All pieces and exercises are specially composed by Vandre. There are pitch drills to establish chord patterns and tonality, and rhythm drills are done in a pitched context. No minor melodies are included. In the unison book some pieces are accompanied, but all the part-book exercises are meant to be sung a cappella. The drills have no text, but all other examples have text that is both sacred and secular. Sacred text is used in a way that would have been acceptable in the 1950s, when the book was written. Unison, two-part, and SSA books are all in treble clef; the three- and four-part books offer bass clef parts. The choral literature is in the book with all pieces written by Vandre.

Method: The pitch system used varies between sol-fa (movable "do"), movable numbers, and both, and in some books no syllable system is mentioned. The inside cover of each book explains Vandre's "down up" system for counting rhythms out loud. At the end of two of the books, he explains why he thinks this system works better and urges teachers to "use it religiously." It is a beat-based system in which each quarter is spoken as "down" and a half note is "down 2" (except in the unison book, where it is "hold 2"). With the exception of the unison book, the books could be used with any pitch or rhythm system. The unison book offers a quick overview of some music fundamentals as well as an explanation of Vandre's counting system. The other, more advanced books offer drills in modulation and chromatics but with no explanations (or syllables).

Evaluation: No evaluation materials or suggestions are provided. The approach is not really compatible with graded assessment.

Distinguishing Features: Vandre's beat-based counting system seems difficult to use, and the logic is hard to understand (e.g., $\frac{4}{4}$ is "down down down down"; $\frac{6}{8}$ is "down down down down down down"). The approach to both pitch and rhythm is not consistent among books despite their being part of the same series. The musical material is of appropriate difficulty, but the texts and sentiments are quite dated, as is the free use of sacred text. There is little information for the teacher on how to use the books. The unison book is intended to be used for either vocal or instrumental (flutophone/tonette) sight-reading.

THE SIGHT-SINGER
Audrey Snyder
CPP Belwin

Two-Part and Three-Part Mixed Voices, volume 1 (1993)/volume 2 (1994)	Teacher ($29.95); Student ($3.95); Cassette/CD($25.00/$49.95)
Unison and Two-Part Treble Voices, volume 1 (1993)/volume 2 (1994)	Teacher ($29.95); Student ($3.95); Cassette/CD ($25.00/$49.95)

Level and Sequence: The series was designed for middle school/junior high singers with little previous training. Ranges fit changing voices well. The unison and two-part editions are almost identical in sequence to the mixed-voice edition but geared more toward upper elementary with all treble clefs and limited to two parts. The books are very carefully sequenced to introduce one new element at a time, with a number of practice examples for each new concept.

Content: Many exercises are specially composed, but they are interspersed with folk tunes in two- and three-part settings and compositions by the author. Some rhythm-only exercises when new material is introduced. Most exercises feature a complete musical context but simplify the rhythm when pitch is challenging, and vice versa. Natural minor is introduced at the very end of volume 1 and picked up again early in volume 2 along with the introduction of the blues scale and irregular meters. All of the exercises in the two- and three-part edition feature both clefs from the beginning. Exercises range from unison to three parts. There is a nice balance of text and no text exercises, and the book teaches expressive markings and other musical symbols throughout the sequence. All of the exercises are meant to be read unaccompanied. The accompaniment tapes are for use after the first reading. No accompaniments are written out for the teacher to play. There is no correlated literature other than the author's own short compositions.

Method: The sequence is strongly sound-before-symbol, using movable "do" and minor "la" solfège along with Kodàly's rhythm syllables. For the teacher, pages 46–49 in volume 1 offer standard sight-singing sequences similar to examples found in chapter 4 of this book, which teach students how to approach a score when reading. Music fundamentals are introduced concept-by-concept as needed to develop reading skills.

Evaluation: No evaluation material is included in the text and the volumes are not divided into levels, making it challenging to decide when to evaluate student progress. However, the review and practice examples interspersed throughout the text might provide assessment opportunities.

Distinguishing Features: Lots of information for teachers on teaching strategies for introducing new concepts and mastering skills. Very clear and engaging layout for students and teachers. "Mystery" tunes are familiar tunes that students must use their reading skills to identify, though there are hints (e.g., Canine Mystery Tune is "Bingo"). Accompaniment cassette includes accompaniments for every exercise to add musical interest to the singing. Large charts that illustrate different scales (with a harmonic exercise) and a keyboard layout are provided to help teach music fundamentals.

SONGS FOR SIGHT-SINGING
Mary Henry and Marilyn Jones
Southern Music Company

Volume 1 (1987)	High School SATB ($7.50); High School SSA ($7.95); High School TTB ($4.95); High School–Junior High SAB ($7.95); Junior High SATB ($6.95); Junior High S(S)A ($6.50); Junior High T(T)B ($6.95)
Volume 2 (1995)	Same voicings all $7.95

Level and Sequence: The books are intended for middle school/junior high through high school. The three- and four-part pieces generally move from easy to advanced as you progress through each book, though there is not a wide range of difficulty levels within each book. None of the pieces are so difficult as to qualify as advanced.

Content: Each book represents a collection of music composed specifically for sight-singing contests and designed to be appropriate for the voice ranges and skill levels of junior high and high school choirs. The books are graded in the sense that junior high SAB is easier than junior high

SATB, which is easier than high school SATB. Only the last three pieces in the high school SATB collection are in minor mode. All pieces are unaccompanied with text and very few accidentals. Rhythm can get complicated in some pieces that include eighth- and sixteenth-note runs, mixed meters, and two against three. All of the examples include text and all the other expressive markings one would associate with choral literature as opposed to exercises.

Method: The material can be used with any method. The books contain music but no instructional material.

Evaluation: No guidelines for assessment are given, but the materials were designed to be used with the Texas University Interscholastic League (UIL) large-group sight-singing contest.

Distinguishing Features: Having a collection of graded and accessible choral literature for use in reading practice can be invaluable, and 19 choral pieces for $7.50 is a bargain, though few of the pieces are really suitable for concert performance. The fact that these pieces were actually used in sight-singing contests gives them a certain authenticity for group reading instruction. They may not be difficult enough for a really advanced group.

SUCCESSFUL SIGHT-SINGING
Nancy Telfer
Neil A. Kjos Music Company
Volume 1 (1992)   Teacher ($19.95); Student ($6.95)
Volume 2 (1992)   Teacher ($19.95); Student ($6.95)

Level and Sequence: The books are designed for middle school intermediate or beginning high school or adult choirs. The ranges fit middle school needs very well, but the lack of repetition at each difficulty level may create problems for younger singers. Graded in difficulty with gradual pitch changes but moves relatively fast with regard to rhythm.

Content: The exercises start with "do–sol," then add "mi" to complete the triad. Eventually "re" and "la" are added to complete a pentatonic scale, but exercises focus on triadic harmony. Minor is introduced in volume 1's exercise 43 soon after "la" solfège. The pitch sequencing is very gradual and logical, with lots of repetition. Part singing is introduced right away in volume 1's exercise 2. Rhythm moves fairly quickly compared with other sight-singing methods, and all new time values are introduced in a pitched context, with few separate rhythm exercises. For example, volume 1's exercise 4 is a two-part example that includes quarter note, eighth note, and quarter rest in a mixed meter of $\frac{3}{4}$ and $\frac{4}{4}$. Most of the exercises are a cappella, though some pieces are accompanied. There is correlated literature written or arranged by Telfer and connected directly to the "Milestone" levels within each volume.

Method: The teacher's manual offers an overview of the organization and philosophy behind the series. There are teaching tips presented with each new exercise regarding sight-singing, but also warm-ups, score marking, and other choral skills. The author clearly believes in contextualizing reading; no separation of pitch and rhythm because it "handicaps" the singers. The book is based on movable "do" and minor "la" for pitch reading but no rhythm system, just spoken on "dah." The introduction also suggests that "the singers should read the notes and the words at the same time the first time through" (p. 8). It is not clear what role solfège plays in the reading process beyond being used in warm-ups. Theory information is integrated into the sequence of exercises as needed and reviewed regularly.

Evaluation: No materials or guidelines for evaluation are provided. However, materials are organized by volume, and levels within each volume are referred to as "Milestones." Since Milestones signal the introduction of some new concept (e.g., milestone 4: "Accidentals"), they could be used as opportunities to assess mastery of previously learned concepts.

Distinguishing Features: Overall the books provide an extremely contemporary approach, which introduces mixed meters and challenging rhythmic material very early on and deals with minor mode earlier than most. A very choral approach in terms of the continual use of part singing. All exercises and pieces have text, which is very unusual. For younger or less-experienced groups, there may not be enough repetition at each step before introducing new musical material. Given the level of rhythmic challenges in the book, it is somewhat surprising that no rhythm-reading system is recommended. The student book is very colorful, with "reminders" and "tips" on choral singing interspersed with new musical material. However, the pages of the student book are very full of material, making them visually kind of "busy." Consequently, directions, new material, and even the notation are sometimes hard to find and to follow.

VOCAL CONNECTIONS
Ruth Whitlock
Southern Music Company (1992)
Teacher's Kit ($49.95); 5-pack of grids ($19.95); 5-pack of exercises ($19.95); Audio Lessons ($9.95 each)

Level and Sequence: The author states that the series was field-tested with elementary school through university classrooms. The series is based somewhat loosely on Edwin Gordon's "Music Learning Theory." The book moves from echoing patterns on neutral syllables, to reading solfège in grid notation, to reading traditional notation using solfège. The goal is to develop audiation, Gordon's term, which "approximates the concept of inner hearing" (p. 1).

Content: The content is organized chordally, beginning with "do–mi–sol" patterns and moving to chords built on "sol," "fa," and so forth. The first five exercises are presented aurally on a tape. For the first lesson, the teacher is instructed to have the students listen through once and audiate, then listen again and echo. The author recommends working on only one lesson per week, so the goal is to internalize the patterns. After lesson 1, students listen and echo right away, first in the large group and then in small groups and individually. The grids are introduced in lesson 5 with the idea that students will first echo the patterns aurally, then once that is mastered read the same patterns again from the grid. All of the exercises have a harmonic accompaniment in a variety of styles to give at least some musical context for the singing. There are no pieces or exercises with text. No recommendations are made regarding how these lessons could be integrated with rehearsals of the literature.

Method: This is most definitely a method-centered approach that is not compatible with other traditional approaches to teaching music reading. The sequences are designed to build up a student's vocabulary of internal patterns, which is very consistent with Gordon's approach (see chapter 3). Yet Whitlock's approach differs from Gordon in several important ways: 1) the patterns are sung in the harmonic context of an accompaniment; 2) all of the students sing all of the patterns; and 3) there is no systematic attention to rhythm sequencing. Dr. Whitlock was aware of these discrepancies, as was Dr. Gordon, who is said to have approved of her ideas. Movable "do" solfège is used for pitch reading, and any rhythm system can be used, though Gordon has his own. There is no theory information provided. In fact, the book states emphatically: "Do not teach theory!"

Evaluation: There are suggestions for evaluation on page 7 using the audio lessons and a tape recorder to assess student progress.

Distinguishing Features: The audio lessons feature tonal patterns sung by either a male or female voice with piano accompaniment. The tapes are recorded split-track so that a teacher could use the tapes in a voice-only or piano-only presentation. The late Dr. Whitlock was an outstanding teacher and a great admirer of Edwin Gordon. While these materials are an intriguing approach to developing inner hearing, they would be difficult to pick up and use effectively without some kind of special training in this approach.

SUMMARY CHART OF PUBLISHED MATERIALS

Figure 8.1 allows a teacher to locate quickly materials that fit a particular pedagogical need. The chart is organized alphabetically and indicates the page number on which the full review appears in this text. If letters or dots appear in a particular category, it indicates that the book offers

FIGURE 8.1. CHART OF SIGHT-SINGING MATERIALS.

Sight-Singing Books	Pitch System	Rhythm System	Separate	Unison	Multipart	Minor	Bass Clef	Teaching Tips	Theory	Text	Evaluation	Page Number
Choir Trainer Series	MD/N	O/A	◗	◗	●	●	●					133
The Choral Approach to Sight Singing	MD	S	●	●	●	◗	●	●	●	●		152
Choral Connections	MD/N	A	●	●	●	●	●	●	●	●	●	134
Choral Reader	MD	A	◗	●	◗	●	●		◗	◗		136
Essential Musicianship	A	A	●	●	●	●	●	●	●	●	◗	137
The Folk Song Sight Singing Series	MD/A	A		●	◗	●			◗			138
The Independent Singer	MD/N	A		●	◗		●	●	●			139
Introduction to Sight-singing & The Choral Sight Singer	MD	C		●	●		●	●	●	◗	◗	140
Jenson Sight Singing Course	MD	C	●	●	●	●	●	●	●		◗	142
Keys to Sight Reading Success	MD/N	A	◗	●	●	◗	●					143
Kodály Choral Method	MD	S		●	●	●			◗		◗	144
Masterworks Sight-Singing Collection	MD	A	●	●	●	◗						146
Melodia	A	A		●	●	●	●					148
Music Reading Unlimited	MD/N	C	◗	●	●	●	●	●	●		◗	149
Patterns of Sound	MD	S	●	●	●	◗		●	●	●		151
Sight Reading Fun Series	MD/A	O/A	◗	●	●		●			◗	●	154
The Sight-singer	MD	S	◗	●	●	●	●	●	●	●	◗	155
Sight-singing for SSA	MD	S	●	●	●	◗		●	●	●		153
Songs for Sight-singing	A	A			●	◗	●			●		156
Successful Sight-Singing	MD	A	◗	●	●	●	●	●	●	●	◗	157
Vocal Connections	MD	A	●	●			●	●	●		●	158

● = Full amount of content provided
◗ = Some content provided
= No content provided

that particular content. Half-dots mean a "less than average" amount is offered. There is no category for level because most of the books offer multiple levels of difficulty. The categories are as follows:

1. Pitch System: The book uses movable "do" (MD), fixed "do" (FD), numbers (N), other (O), or all (A). "All" means that the book can be used with any system.
2. Rhythm System: The book uses counting (C), syllables (S), other (O), or all (A).
3. Separate: The book offers some exercises that feature pitch or rhythm alone.
4. Unison: The book offers some exercises or melodies in unison.
5. Multipart: The book offers at least some exercises or songs in two or more parts.
6. Minor: The book introduces minor scales at some point.
7. Bass Clef: The book offers at least some exercises or songs with bass clef.
8. Teaching Tips: The book offers information on how to teach certain concepts.
9. Theory: The book provides the teacher or student with information and teaching material for music fundamentals (keys, meters, etc.).
10. Text: The book offers exercises or songs with text.
11. Evaluation: The book is structured in a way that would be compatible with regular student evaluation.

CONCLUSION

The majority of choral teachers who responded to the Web survey reported using materials they created themselves, but published sight-singing materials do offer several benefits. Though the initial investment is high, the materials can last for many years. Unlike many textbooks, sight-singing materials do not often need to be updated or revised, though some song material with text can become dated. Having a resource that includes a graded series of exercises and information on music fundamentals and even vocal technique can provide a certain continuity to a beginning choral experience. It allows the teacher to establish a definite level of achievement for students who have completed a particular published "course." Many of the authors of these books are or were experienced and successful sight-singing teachers. Though no book fits the individual needs of every program, finding a text that fits one's teaching style provides a degree of structure to the sight-singing curriculum, particularly at the early stages.

While few of the books offered specific evaluation materials, many are organized in such a way that teacher-created assessments can easily be inserted at various points. By using a published introductory text the teacher has a set of exercises from which to teach and then can add or delete as circumstances demand from year to year. In subsequent years, octavos and more advanced reading materials can be added to the library to provide challenges at higher levels. For example, finding a set of used hymnals or a Bach chorale collection provides hours of quality reading material. Building a good sight-singing library, like a good choral library, is something that happens over a number of years as budgets allow and can pay dividends in terms of the quality and consistency of the sight-singing training.

Appendix

Web Survey Contributor List

The following individuals were among the 178 people who contributed to this book by participating in the Web survey. I gratefully acknowledge the participation of these dedicated teachers.

Janice Anderson-Chapin
Allan Andrews
Sandra Augsburger
Debby Barkey
Cindy Bauchspies
Sophia M. Beharrie
Timothy M. Black
Corey Blaker
Nancy Boehm
Christopher Borges
Robert Bowden
Daniel Boyle
Gloria J. Brandt
Athena Brooks
Twyla Brunson
R. Marie Burns
Dr. Kerry P. Burtis
Tim Carpenter
Charles E. Claiborne
Gregory Cleveland
Susan Coburn
Jill J. Couto
Anne L. Davis
Thomas P. Davis

O. David Deitz
Gabriel Dumitrescu
Joe Fisher
Jennie Flicker
John H. Fohner
Dr. Frederic Ford
Peggy Forstad
Robert C. Fullerton, Jr.
Erin Gabriel
Kathleen Gabriele
Tina B. Gill
Carolyn A. Gipe
Margaret Green
Adrian Guerra
Rhonda Hawley
Rev. J. Mazie Henderson
Susan Hinrichs
Steven P. Hinz
Richard Hintze
Larry Hook
Scott A. Houston
Amy Johns
Alexa Johnson
Bob Jones

Paula Joyner-Clinard
Gloria Juan
Suzanne Marie Kane
Gordon S. Krauspe
Jennifer D. Krinke
Ann Marie Kyle
John Lampe
Marsha Larson
Scott Leaman
Debby Lyttle
MaryClare Martin
Thomas R. Martin
Dr. James T. Masullo, Jr.
Elspeth Maynard
Cynthia G. Mayo
Donna McCommon
Stephen McDonough
Richard Messenger
Catherine A. Miller
Suzanne Mudge
Patrick Murphy
Rebecca Ng
Janice G. Noblitt
Aaron R. Olson
Monica Paonessa
Russell J. Parker
Jeffery S. Patrick, Sr
Robert C. Paugh

Judy Penick
Anthony G. Ransfer
Carol Richardi
Peter Schleif
Deb Schnitkey
Lori Schrock
Kathleen Spadafino
Martha Springetead
Tim Sterner
Bradley R. Taylor
Nelba Thomas
Frank Timmerman
Bette-Jeanne Townsend
Brianne Turgeon
David Twiss
Rebecca Walker
Rondal Wallace
Lewis Walling
Matthew Wanner
Gary Weidenaar
Kenneth Roger Westerman
Steven Weston
Steve White
Lynn Whitescarver
Lou Williams-Wimberly
Dale Witte
Lisa Yozviak

Notes

PART I: WHY TEACH SIGHT-SINGING?

1. A History of Sight-Singing Instruction in the United States

1. John Playford's *Brief Introduction to the Skill of Music* published in England in 1679 provided much of the theoretical information (and some of the music) for most early American tune books.

2. For more resources on shape note singing and its history, see John Bealle's comprehensive bibliography at http://fasola.org/bibliography/index.html. Information regarding current Sacred Harp (a group that follows the shape note tradition) singing activities can be found at http://fasola.org/.

3. It is interesting to note that one year later Sarah Glover published "Scheme for Rendering Psalmody Congregational" in Norwich, England. Glover's method also featured a seven-syllable movable "do" and the learning of syllables prior to introducing the rules of notation. Glover's method was extremely influential in the development of Tonic Sol-fa.

4. There were some graded method books prior to the *National Music Course*, such as Jepson's *New Standard Music Reader* and Loomis's *Progressive Music Lessons*, that were smaller in scope and more local in influence than Luther Mason's series. For more information on nineteenth-century songbooks see John (1954, pp. 103–118).

5. Both Birge (1928) and J. A. Keene (1982) state that Luther Mason was the first advocate of the song method, but clearly Lowell Mason was an advocate of the same rote-before-note pedagogy espoused in the song method long before the *National Music Course* was published. Birge and Keene also indicate that Luther Mason's approach was based on Tonic Sol-fa and the Galin-Paris-Chevé notation. While Mason was clearly aware of these approaches, his method seems more closely allied to that of Lowell Mason. In the preface to *The New First Music Reader: Preparatory to Sight-Singing* (1886), he speaks of the influence of Pestalozzi and Hohmann. In addition, he makes a clear distinction between his time names and those of "Chévré" (*sic*) and his solfège syllables use "si" for the seventh scale degree instead of the "ti" favored by Tonic Sol-fa.

6. On a personal note, my father graduated from Omaha Central High School in 1949. Though he played in the band, he mentioned that at his twentieth reunion he was singing next to the choir "stars" and realized that many of them could not read music.

2. What Research Offers Teachers

1. May's results were based on the responses of 292 directors. While this is a fairly large number, it represented only 22% of his original sample, so the possibility exists that results were biased toward teachers who favored sight-singing.

2. The survey URL is: http://faculty.washington.edu/demorest/survey.cgi.

PART II. HOW TO TEACH SIGHT-SINGING

1. Interestingly enough, after very thoroughly pointing out that *every* solmization system has flaws, Winnick reiterates his belief that one right way can be found:"I have written this article to express my strong conviction and hope that inquiry and intensive examination of all methods will lead, not only to further public discussion, but to a growing conviction that there *is* a superior method" (p. 30).

3. Systems and Methods of Instruction

1. Tonic Sol-fa as used by Glover and Curwen was more than just a syllable system. Following Pestalozzi's dictate of "the thing before the sign," which had influenced Lowell Mason, there was a clear sequence of moving from imitation, to simple patterns on a chart, to part singing, and finally to standard notation.

2. Curwen originally presented the sol-fa syllables with standard notation, but the popularity of his shorthand notation, combined with the lower cost of printing only text, led him to abandon the standard notation connection. This connection has been revived in the *New Curwen Method*.

3. Numbers do appear in both Lowell Mason's and Luther Mason's method books in the 1800s but were probably used much earlier. W. H. Cummings in his response to McNaught's 1893 address (see McNaught, 1893) claims that numbers were included along with notes and sol-fa syllables in a book published in 1560 in Lyon, though no title or author is given.

4. A. Bentley suggested this system, based on movable "do," in response to a proposal by H. Siler (1956) for an international fixed solfège system called "safa."

5. Another major elementary music education method not mentioned here is Orff-Schulwerk. It is excluded here because while music literacy is a component of Orff-Schulwerk, sight-singing is not a primary goal. The Orff method focuses on exploration and improvisation that used pitched percussion along with rhythmic chanting, body percussion, and movement. Rhythm literacy is achieved by moving from rhythmic chanting, to graphic notation, and then to standard notation, with a focus on recording students' own musical ideas. Solfège, when it is used, is movable "do" introduced gradually through known songs.

6. Kodály's ideas about music teaching are often called the Kodály philosophy or Kodály concept. While he presents principles for sequencing instruction

and choosing materials, there is perhaps more flexibility in approach than is typical of a "method." For more information on the Kodály concept see the recommended readings at the end of the chapter.

7. Gordon is well known as a researcher and creator of standardized music aptitude tests such as the *Primary Measures of Music Audiation*. His ideas on music pedagogy grew out of his explorations into musical aptitude.

8. Dr. Ruth Whitlock's *Vocal Connections* choral sight-singing book is Gordon-based, but the late Dr. Whitlock admitted that many of the activities do not strictly adhere to the learning sequences approach found in other materials created by Gordon. While Gordon's method is not used as frequently with choral directors (3 out of 178 in the Web survey), I have seen it used in a middle school choral rehearsal. The director took about ten minutes after warm-ups to echo pitch and rhythm patterns on a neutral syllable and then solfège, both group and individual, marking the students on a clipboard in the Evaluation Mode. In the class I observed, there was no connection between these exercises and the rest of the rehearsal, but the director said she felt it was really helping the students' musicianship.

4. Sight-Singing Lesson Models

1. The bingo cards can be made up entirely of solfège or rhythm patterns or can be a combination, as shown in figure 4.17. If the card has a combination of materials, it is probably wise to have all of the patterns under each letter be of the same type. Thanks to my student Susan Jones, who introduced me to the idea of musical bingo.

2. Thanks to Leann Banton Rozema at Kellogg Middle School for introducing me to one version of this game.

References

Bargar, R. R. (1964). A study of music reading: Groundwork for research in the development of training programs (Doctoral dissertation, Ohio State University, Columbus). *Dissertation Abstracts International, 25,* 2416A.

Bennett, Peggy. (1984). Tricks, masks, and camouflage: Is imitation passing for music reading? *Music Educators Journal, 71*(3), 62–63, 65–69.

Bentley, A. (1959). Fixed or movable do? *Journal of Research in Music Education, 7,* 163–168.

Bertalot, John. (1993). *Five wheels to successful sight-singing.* Minneapolis: Augsburg Fortress.

Birge, Edward B. (1928). *History of public school music in the United States.* Boston: Oliver Ditson.

Blum, B. E. (1971). Solmization and pitch notation in nineteenth-century American school music textbooks. *Journal of Research in Music Education, 19,* 443–452.

Boyle, J. D., & K. V. Lucas. (1990). The effect of context on sightsinging. *Bulletin of the Council for Research in Music Education, (106),* 1–9.

Brendell, J. K. (1996). Time use, rehearsal activity and student off-task behavior during the initial minutes of high school choral rehearsals. *Journal of Research in Music Education, 44,* 6–14.

Brinson, B. A. (1996). *Choral music methods and materials: Developing successful choral programs.* (Chapter 4.) New York: Schirmer.

Carey, W. (1959). *A survey of the sight reading ability of senior students in nine Kansas high schools.* Unpublished master's thesis, University of Kansas, Lawrence.

Choksy, L. (1999a). *The Kodály method I: Comprehensive music education* (3d ed.). Upper Saddle River, NJ: Prentice Hall.

Choksy, L. (1999b). *The Kodály method II: Folksong to masterwork.* Upper Saddle River, NJ: Prentice Hall.

Colley, B. (1987). A comparison of syllabic methods for improving rhythm literacy. *Journal of Research in Music Education, 35,* 221–235.

Colwell, R. (1963). An investigation of musical achievement among vocal students, vocal-instrumental students, and instrumental students. *Journal of Research in Music Education, 11,* 123–130.

Daniels, R. D. (1986). Relationships among selected factors and the sight-reading ability of high school mixed choirs. *Journal of Research in Music Education, 34,* 279–289.

Daniels, R. D. (1988). Sight-reading instruction in the choral rehearsal. *Update: Applications of Research in Music Education, 6*(2), 22–24.

Demorest, S. M. (1998a). Improving sight-singing performance in the choral ensemble: The effect of individual testing. *Journal of Research in Music Education, 46,* 182–192.

Demorest, S. M. (1998b). Sight-singing in the secondary choral ensemble: A review of the research. *Bulletin of the Council for Research in Music Education, 137,* 1–15.

Demorest, S. M., & W. V. May. (1995). Sight-singing instruction in the choral ensemble: Factors related to individual performance. *Journal of Research in Music Education, 43,* 156–167.

Dwiggins, R. (1984). Teaching sight-reading in the high school chorus. *Update: Applications of Research in Music Education, 2*(2), 8–11.

Ernst, K. D. (1957). A study of certain practices in music education in school systems of cities over 150,000 population. *Journal of Research in Music Education, 5,* 23–30.

Evans, J. (1994). *Practica Musica* (Version 3.53) [Computer software]. Kirkland, WA: Ars Nova Software.

Gagne, R. M. (1965). *The conditions of learning.* New York: Holt, Rinehart & Winston.

Galin, Pierre. (1983). *Rationale for a new way of teaching music* (from Exposition d'une Nouvelle methode). (B. Rainbow, Trans.). Kilkenny, Ireland: Boethius Press (original work published 1818).

Gaston, E. Thayer. (1940). *A study of the trends of attitudes toward music in school children with a study of the methods used by high school students in sight-reading music.* Unpublished doctoral dissertation, University of Kansas, Lawrence, 1940.

Goolsby, T. W. (1994a). Eye movement in music reading: Effects of reading ability, notational complexity, and encounters. *Music Perception, 12,* 77–96.

Goolsby, T. W. (1994b). Profiles of processing: Eye movements during sightreading. *Music Perception, 12,* 97–123.

Gordon, Edwin E. (1997). *Learning sequences in music: Skill, content, and patterns.* Chicago: GIA Publications.

Grunow, R. F., & Edwin E. Gordon. (1989). Jump right in: The instrumental series (Teacher's guide). Chicago: G.I.A. Publications.

Hales, B. (1961). A study of music reading programs in high school choruses in the Rocky Mountain states (Doctoral dissertation, University of Oregon, Eugene, 1961). *Dissertation Abstracts International, 22,* 2416.

Hammer, H. (1961). An experimental study of the use of the tachistoscope in the teaching of melodic sightsinging (Doctoral Dissertation, University of Colorado, Boulder, 1961). *Dissertation Abstracts International, 22,* 3690–3691.

Hansen, L. A. (1961). A study of score reading ability of musicians. *Journal of Research in Music Education, 9,* 147–156.

Henke, Herbert H. (1984). The application of Émile Jaques-Dalcroze's Solfège-rhythmique to the choral rehearsal. *Choral Journal, 24*(5), 11–14.

Henry, M., & S. M. Demorest. (1994). Individual sight-singing achievement in successful choral ensembles: A preliminary study. *Update: Applications of Research in Music Education, 13*(1), 4–8.

Hodges, D. (1992). The acquisition of music reading skills. In R. Colwell (Ed.), *Handbook of research on music teaching and learning* (pp. 466–471). New York: Schirmer.

Hutton, D. (1953). A comparative study of two methods of teaching sight singing in the fourth grade. *Journal of Research in Music Education, 1*, 119–125.

Hylton, J. (1995). *Comprehensive choral music education.* Englewood Cliffs, NJ: Prentice Hall.

Jackson, George Pullen. (1933). *White spirituals in the southern uplands: The story of the fasola folk, their songs, singings, and "buckwheat notes."* Chapel Hill: University of North Carolina Press. Reprint. New York, NY: Dover, 1965.

John, R. W. (1954). Nineteenth century graded vocal series. *Journal of Research in Music Education, 2*, 103–118.

Johnson, G. J. B. (1987). *A descriptive study of the pitch-reading methods and the amount of time utilized to teach sight-singing by high school choral teachers in the north central region of the American Choral Directors Association.* Unpublished master's thesis, University of Nebraska, Lincoln.

Keenan-Takagi, K. (2000). Embedded assessment in the middle school choral ensemble. *Music Educators Journal, 86*(4), 42–46, 63.

Keene, J. A. (1982). *A history of music education in the United States.* Hanover, NH: University Press of New England.

Kegerreis, R. I. (1970). History of the high school a cappella choir. *Journal of Research in Music Education, 18*, 319–329.

Klemish, J. J. (1970). A comparative study of two methods of teaching music reading to first-grade children. *Journal of Research in Music Education, 18*, 355–364.

Knuth, W. E. (1933). *The construction and validation of music tests designed to measure certain aspects of sight-reading.* Unpublished doctoral dissertation, University of California, Berkeley.

Kyme, G. H. (1960). An experiment in teaching children to read music with shape notes. *Journal of Research in Music Education, 8*, 3–8.

Law, Andrew. (1803). *The art of singing in three parts* (4th ed.). Cambridge, MA: W. Hilliard.

Law, Andrew. (1812). *Select harmony.* Philadelphia: Robert & William Carr.

Lucas, K. V. (1994). Contextual condition and sightsinging achievement of middle school choral students. *Journal of Research in Music Education, 42*, 203–216.

Luce, J. R. (1965). Sight-reading and ear-playing abilities as related to instrumental music students. *Journal of Research in Music Education, 13*, 101–109.

Martin, B. A. (1991). Effects of hand signs, syllables, and letters on first graders' acquisition of tonal skills. *Journal of Research in Music Education, 39*, 161–170.

Mason, Lowell (1837). *Manual of the Boston Academy of Music, for instruction in the elements of vocal music on the system of Pestalozzi* (2d ed.). Boston: J. H. Wilkins & R. B. Carter.

Mason, Luther W. (1886). *The new first music reader: Preparatory to sight-singing*. Boston: Ginn.

May, J. A. (1993). A description of current practices in the teaching of choral melody reading in the high schools of Texas (Doctoral dissertation, University of Houston, 1993). *Dissertation Abstracts International, 54*, 856A.

May, W. V., & C. A. Elliott. (1980). Relationships among ensemble participation, private instruction, and aural skill development. *Journal of Research in Music Education, 28*, 155–161.

McCoy, C. W. (1989). Basic training: Working with inexperienced choirs. *Music Educators Journal, 75*(8), 42–45.

McHose, A. I., & R. N. Tibbs. (1945). *Sight-singing manual* (2d ed.). New York: Appleton-Century-Crofts.

McNaught, W. G. (1893). The history and uses of the sol-fa syllables. *Proceedings of the Musical Association, 19*, 35–51.

More, B. E. (1985). Sight singing and ear training at the university level: A case for the use of Kodály's system of relative solmization. *Choral Journal, 25*(8), 9–22.

Music Educators National Conference (with CNAEA). (1994). *National standards for arts education: What every young American should know and be able to do in the arts*. Reston, VA: Author.

Musicware. (1997). *Music Lab Melody* (Version 3.0d) [Computer software]. Redmond, WA: Music Lab Systems.

Nolker, B. (1996). *The relationship between Missouri state large ensemble sight-reading rating and the individual's sight-singing success: A pilot study*. Unpublished manuscript.

O'Brien, J. P. (1969). An experimental study of the use of shape notes in developing sight singing (Doctoral dissertation, University of Colorado, Boulder, 1969). *Dissertation Abstracts International, 31*, 1313A.

Pemberton, Carol Ann. (1985). *Lowell Mason: His life and work*. Ann Arbor: UMI Research Press.

Phillips, K. H. (1996). Teaching singers to sight-read. *Teaching Music, 3*(6), 32–33.

Ritter, F. L. (1883). *Music in America*. New York: Charles Scribner's Sons.

Rodeheaver, R. E. (1972). An investigation of the vocal sight-reading ability of college freshman music majors (Doctoral dissertation, University of Oklahoma, Norman, 1972). *Dissertation Abstracts International, 33/03*, 1190A.

Shuler, S. C. (1996). The effects of the National Standards on assessment (and vice versa). In *Aiming for excellence: The impact of the standards movement on music education*. Reston, VA: Music Educators National Conference.

Siler, H. (1956). Toward an international solfeggio. *Journal of Research in Music Education, 4*, 40–43.

Sloboda, J. A. (1984). Experimental studies of musical reading: A review. *Music Perception, 2*, 222–236.

Smith, T. A. (1987). Solmization: A tonic for healthy musicianship. *Choral Journal, 28*(1), 16–23.

Szabo, C. E. (1992). A profile of ten high school choral directors and their activities during one week (Doctoral dissertation, Kent State University, 1992). *Dissertation Abstracts International, 53*, 2730A.

Szönyi, E. (1973). *Kodály's principles in practice: an approach to music education through the Kodály method.* (J. Weissman, Trans.). New York: Boosey & Hawkes.

Tucker, D. W. (1969). Factors related to musical reading ability of senior high school students participating in choral groups (Doctoral dissertation, University of California, Berkeley, 1969). *Dissertation Abstracts International, 31,* 2427A.

Winnick, W. (1987). Hybrid methods in sight-singing. *Choral Journal, 28*(1), 24–30.

Zimmerman, C. R. (1962). Relationship of musical environment to choral sight-reading ability (Doctoral dissertation, University of Oregon, Eugene, 1962). *Dissertation Abstracts International, 24,* 1198.

Index

octavos, 21–22, 28, 127–128, 135, 143, 147, 151, 162

Patterns of Sound, 128, 137, 151–153
Performer 6.01, 114
piano, 25, 32
    as harmonic context, 22
    as a teaching aid, 61, 67, 87, 97
    training and sight-singing success, 24–25, 32

rating scale, 116–117
relative solmization, 38
rote learning, 9–11, 58, 60–65, 96, 100–101, 141
    and Gordon, 56
    and Kodály, 52, 91
rubrics, 117–119, 135

scale step numbers, 9, 11, 40–41, 44, 58
    in published materials, 135, 136, 140, 144, 150, 154
    research on, 21, 28
self-created materials, 21, 28, 127–128
shape notes, 8, 43
Sight Reading Fun Series, 154–155
Sight-singer, The, 128, 155–156
Sight-singing for SSA, 153–154
Sight-Singing with Words, 147–148
singing school, the, 6–8, 9, 12, 18, 39
solfège card game, 85–86

Solfège-rhythmique, 55
solmization. *See* relative solmization; fixed solmization
Songs for Sight-singing, 156–157
Steps to Harmony, 148
St. Olaf College Choir, 13, 14
Successful Sight Singing, 128, 157–158
survey results. *See* Web survey results
systems
    definition of, 21, 37–38
    for reading pitch, 7, 8, 12, 21, 36, 38–47
    for reading rhythm, 7, 11, 21, 48–52
    research on, 21–23, 28

Texas
    research on choirs in, 21–23, 26, 27
    UIL Contest Sight-singing Guidelines, 92, 106–107, 157
time spent teaching sight-singing, 26–27, 30–32, 94
Tonic Sol-fa, 12, 39, 41, 43, 50, 52–53
Tufts, Reverend John, 5–7

Vocal Connections, 158–159

Walter, Reverend Thomas, 5–6
Web survey results, 27–32, 127–130, 161
world music, 17, 19, 100